Svanhild Strøm and Marjun Biskopstø

FAROE
ISLAND KNITS

T|S

TRAFALGAR SQUARE
North Pomfret, Vermont

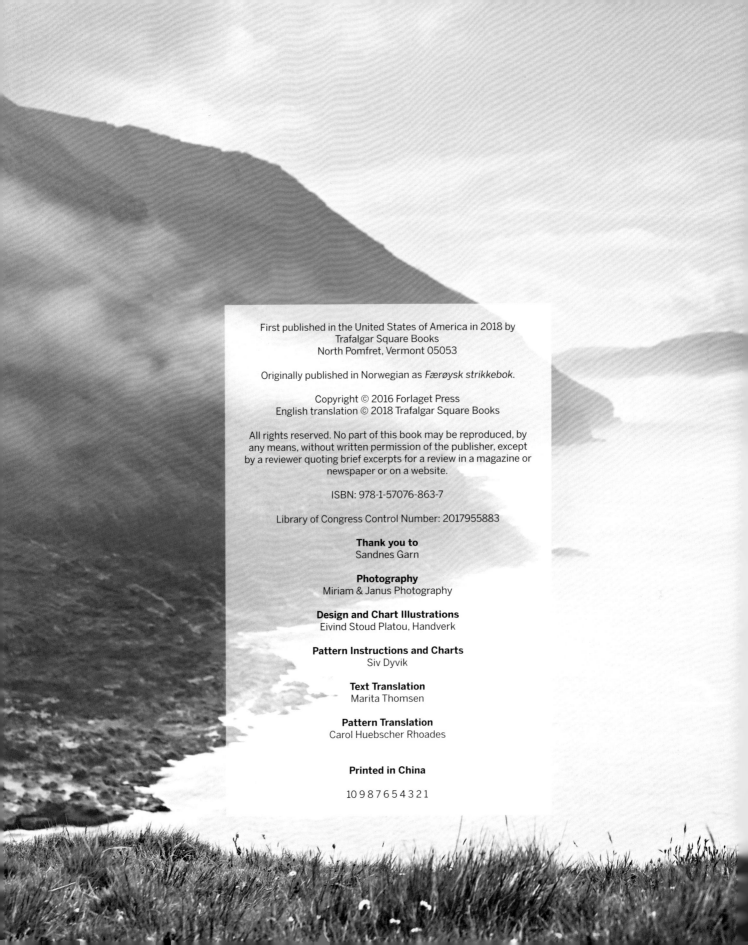

First published in the United States of America in 2018 by
Trafalgar Square Books
North Pomfret, Vermont 05053

Originally published in Norwegian as *Færøysk strikkebok*.

Copyright © 2016 Forlaget Press
English translation © 2018 Trafalgar Square Books

ISBN: 978-1-57076-863-7

Library of Congress Control Number: 2017955883

Thank you to
Sandnes Garn

Photography
Miriam & Janus Photography

Design and Chart Illustrations
Eivind Stoud Platou, Handverk

Pattern Instructions and Charts
Siv Dyvik

Text Translation
Marita Thomsen

Pattern Translation
Carol Huebscher Rhoades

Printed in China

10 9 8 7 6 5 4 3 2 1

CONTENTS

PREFACE

This is a book about Faroese pattern knitting. It is about history, tradition, and especially about the rich pattern heritage of the Faroe Islands.

The Faroese have a deeply rooted knitting culture, and may well hold the world record for number of knitting clubs per capita! Crafters of all ages meet regularly to share ideas and hand down knowledge of traditional handcrafts.

The legacy of Faroese tailor and author Hans Marius Debes inspired us to write this book. The materials he produced in his tireless efforts to preserve Faroese knitting culture are invaluable. Drawing on his book *Føroysk Bindingarmynstur* [Faroese Knitting Motifs], we've designed new garments based on 52 beautiful traditional motifs. We hope to share a glimpse of the wonderful potential we see in pattern knitting!

We are mother and daughter and come from a family where handcrafts have been practiced for generations. Our mother and grandmother, Beinta, was born into a time when thrift was a way of life. Old torn sweaters weren't thrown away; they were cut up and sewn into something different. Every last patch was given new life and reused in colorful rugs, cushions, and curtains. In her home, we grew up surrounded by these beautiful old knitted motifs. Everything she saved through the years became an invaluable resource and source of inspiration for us, and this book has also become a way to remember her.

Above all, we want to spark an interest in Faroese knitting motifs, to increase appreciation of wool as a natural material, and to preserve our cultural legacy. Ultimately, we hope to keep the knitting patterns of the Faroe Islands alive, to honor all those who came before us.

Svanhild and Marjun
Kvívík, Faroe Islands, August 2016

FAROESE KNITTING MOTIFS

Drink my eyes full
Of sea
This morning
And live

~Christian Matras
(Translation by George Johnson)

vi

Føroysk Bindingarmynstur [Faroese Knitting Motifs], written by the tailor Hans Marius Debes, has been a trusted companion throughout my adult life. The idea behind this book is to breathe new life into some of the beautiful knitting patterns he documented.

As I learned more about Hans Marius Debes, I discovered not only 136 different knitting motifs, but also a wealth of stories—lovely tales of a time gone by, a time so very different from my own.

I found inspiration in his detailed descriptions of garments. His portrayals of women, with their central role in handcrafting history, are related with the utmost respect. I've chosen to include some of his stories in this volume; to me they are a precious resource and deserve to be shared.

Sweaters, stockings, and other articles of clothing have been knitted in the Faroe Islands for generations—with Faroese wool. I wanted to see these beautiful motifs worked in yarn from other corners of the world. For the designs in this book, I've chosen a broad selection of yarn from Sandnes Garn, ranging from Norwegian wool to tweed, alpaca, mohair, and silk.

Blue permeates my color universe—probably because the ocean surrounds the Faroe Islands. Here, the sea seems endless. There's no other place in the world where I've found such tranquility and inspiration!

Svanhild
Kvívík, August 2016

HANS MARIUS DEBES

Hans Marius Debes collected old Faroese knitting motifs and published them in the book *Føroysk Bindingarmynstur* [Faroese Knitting Motifs] in 1932. For this work, he was awarded the Danish Royal Medal of Recompense in gold in 1969.

Known as Tailor Debes, he was born in Gjógv, one of the northernmost villages in the Faroes, in 1888, and passed away in 1979. As a boy, he was captivated by handcrafts such as knitting, crochet, and embroidery. All things aesthetic and creative fascinated him—fishing or farming didn't interest him at all.

Debes grew up in the old Faroese farmhouse culture, where woolwork and garment-making were done around the open hearth while older members of the household chanted Faroese ballads and told stories. His grandmother and great-grandfather were eminent storytellers, and Debes also took to the art of storytelling. Later in life, he would pour out his rich knowledge of history, customs, and culture in vivid accounts. His tales, often about priests or the aristocracy, were sprinkled with detailed descriptions of clothing. Today, they're an excellent source of information about both daily life and historic events. His stories were later compiled in the book *Søgur úr gomlum døgum* [Tales of the Old Days].

In his youth, Debes became the apprentice of a tailor named Petersen in the village of Tvøroyi. After six months of study, Debes traveled to Copenhagen to continue his training. He worked at the well-known department stores Illum and Magasin du Nord, as well as at the renowned Moresco. After a few years in Denmark, he returned to the Faroes and set himself up as a master tailor in the capital, Tórshavn. He gained a reputation for quality tailoring, but also had a range of other interests. In his youth he managed to get his hands on a camera; he painted porcelain; and he loved flowers and was skilled at dyeing with plants—a craft he also taught. He had a special interest in the traditional Faroese national costume. After World War II, Debes traveled back to Copenhagen, where he lived for the rest of his life.

It was in conjunction with an exhibition in Copenhagen in 1928 that the story of the book *Føroysk Bindingarmynstur* [Faroese Knitting Motifs] began. Tailor Debes was in charge of the knitted and woven exhibits; one of the pieces shown was a long knitted strip featuring 30 different motifs from the Faroes. The strip had been made a few years earlier in order to preserve some old motifs that were beginning to fade from memory. Queen Alexandrine of Denmark visited the exhibit and was so taken by the patterns that she urged Debes to collect as many old Faroese motifs as possible and publish them, and Debes agreed. In the introduction to the book, he wrote that it had been done in the nick of time, because only the oldest women in the most remote villages remembered most of the patterns he collected.

Tailor Debes collected 125 different motifs for the first edition of the book. A second edition was published in 1949 and it included photos of modern knitted designs. The third and last revised edition dates from 1969 and contains 136 pattern plates. Since then, several more editions have been published.

With the publication of *Føroysk Bindingarmynstur*, knitting in the Faroe Islands changed. In the early 20th century, sweaters knitted in a single color with no patterning were common; after the book was published, a teacher allegedly told Debes, "You, sir, have made all my students stripey." This single sentence clearly illustrates the book's impact.

Danish physician R. K. Rasmussen, who worked in the Faroe Islands in the first half of the 20th century, felt the book was not only significant in terms of knitting history, but for the Faroese style of dress in general. After Tailor Debes brought traditional motifs to everyone's attention, men's sweaters became patterned again, and a wealth of new women's sweater designs appeared. Sweaters for children of all ages were also redesigned. Rasmussen felt that the Faroese people—and women in particular—had quickly become very fond of these motifs.

Debes's Faroese pattern book was his life's work, and for the Faroese it is a national treasure brimming with inspiration for future generations to enjoy. In the Faroes, you'll find the book available in most bookstores, more than 80 years after it was first published.

KNITTING IN THE FAROE ISLANDS

The Faroes are a North Atlantic archipelago, mid-way between Scotland and Iceland. The country consists of 18 islands of volcanic origin, and was previously part of Norway. When Norway's capital moved from Bergen to Christiania (now Oslo), the islands became less important to the Norwegian king. After the 1814 Treaty of Kiel, when Denmark lost Norway to Sweden, the islands were split from the rest of Norway and remained part of Denmark. Since 1948, the Faroe Islands have been a self-governing part of the Kingdom of Denmark, with their own parliament and government. The Faroese also have their own language and their own flag.

The islands are mainly made up of grassy mountains teeming with small flowers. There are no natural forests. Sheep husbandry and the export of wool and knitted garments were once the backbone of the Faroese economy, but they've been displaced by the rise of the fishing industry. Nevertheless, sheep and wool remain central to Faroese traditions and identity, and the Faroese coat of arms is emblazoned with a ram.

Knitting is a cornerstone of Faroese culture. As an old Faroese adage says, "wool is Faroe gold," and even a cursory glance at Faroese knitting history confirms this. Although fewer than 5,000 people lived on the islands in the 17th and 18th centuries, annual exports of knitted woolen stockings numbered in the hundreds of thousands.

The sea has always been central to the Faroese way of life—and to Faroese trade with neighboring countries, since all goods moving in and out of the Faroes must be shipped across the Atlantic. Exports have historically consisted mainly of skins, wool, *vadmal* (fulled woven fabric), fish, feathers, butter, and fish and whale oil, in exchange for imports of wheat, malt, timber, and other processed goods.

No historical account of knitting would be complete without considering nålbinding (single-needle knitting), which may have been common in the Faroe Islands before two-needle knitting arrived. Archaeologists have not uncovered any nålbound garments in the Faroes, but the National Museum in Tórshavn has some needles typically used for nålbinding, preserved from graves at Kvívík and Tjørnuvik, which suggests the Faroese did knit with a single needle for some time, as was common in the rest of the Nordic region.

Knitting as we know it today came to the Faroe Islands in the 16th century. The earliest references to knitting in the Faroes are found in Norwegian documents. The Bergen county ledger lists a pair of old threadbare stockings that were seized after a man was executed, and says they were knitted in the Faroe Islands.

Written Faroese sources refer to the value of stockings as an export product. The prices of goods for export were fixed during a parliamentary session in 1584, and records list the prices of hides, wool, *vadmal*, and stockings. *Moorit* brown stockings fetched five hides, while white stockings were worth four.

The export of woolen stockings was critical to the Faroese economy in the Middle Ages. In order to increase production, Scottish spinning wheels were imported to the Faroes in the late 17th century. A man and a woman were brought in from the Shetland Islands to teach the Faroese how to use them. This new technique boosted stocking production, and stockings overtook *vadmal* as the prime export product. These changes in production also led to a degree of social change. Not everyone had the equipment or the space to produce woven goods, but anyone who could get some wool could knit stockings to sell.

Unfortunately, the increase in production soon led to oversupply; the Faroese were knitting too many stockings. By 1683, it was estimated that it would take three years to sell one year's supply of stockings. Prices tumbled, and the piles of unsold stockings stored in Copenhagen began to grow. Moths got into these stores, and in the first half of the 18th century, a total of 177,000 pairs had to be destroyed. However, production continued, and stockings remained the main export product for the Faroes throughout the 18th century. By 1770, over 100,000 pairs of stockings were sold each year, which made up around 98% of all exports from the Faroe Islands. These stockings were sold in northern

1

Europe and were a popular choice for uniforms for soldiers and sailors.

Everyone who needed or wanted a little extra income was knitting stockings, but not everyone owned land or kept sheep. This led to a spike in people traveling through Faroese villages to beg for wool. In order to stamp out this problem, the authorities enacted a new law on bonded labor, which became known as *Trælalógin*, the Bondage Act. It stipulated that the working classes and the poor had a duty to take on work at farms. Anyone failing to do so would be punished. Subsequently, the law was altered to bar landless couples from marrying until they'd served on a farm for a period of four years. The farmers, in conjunction with the authorities, alleged that people were needed to farm the land, and the stated aim of the legislation was to curb begging and reduce poverty—but many bonded laborers on farms were ordered to knit instead, because it was so profitable.

Stocking production fell in the 19th century, and people began to knit sweaters for export instead. By the end of the 19th century, only a few hundred pairs of stockings were exported annually.

Sweaters were knitted in the Faroes as early as the 17th century. Exactly when pattern knitting began is unknown, but patterned sweaters were common by the late 18th century. That was also when the Faroese started exporting the characteristic *bátsmanstroyggja*—the fisherman's sweater.

By 1805, the supply of knitted fishermen's sweaters exceeded demand, which gave rise to a proposal to sell wool directly, instead of knitted sweaters. The Faroese refused, probably because they used the fine undercoat wool themselves, while the coarser overhair went into fishermen's sweaters to sell.

The quality of the sweaters knitted for sale probably varied. In 1833, detailed guidance was published that set standards for the required number of stitches, measurements, and weight. According to these standards, motifs should be small, with short floats crossing over four stitches at most. Yarns for pattern knitting should be dyed with orchil (lichen), the darker the better. The guidelines also specified how wool should be handled.

Production of fishermen's sweaters lasted throughout the 19th century, and by 1850 it accounted for half of all Faroese exports. However, with the transition from an agrarian economy to industrial fisheries in the 1880s, production shifted to better suit local consumption. The population was booming, and seafarers needed multiple sets of work clothes (including sweaters and mittens) to take on their fishing expeditions.

For some reason, the Faroese fisherman's sweater acquired the name *Islander* ("Icelander") in other countries. In 1898, the Norwegian author Trygve Andersen, on a trip to the Faroe Islands, recounts that "all the famous *Islander* woolen sweaters are knitted here, not in Iceland." To this day, Faroese sweaters are mistakenly known as Icelandic sweaters internationally.

During the 20th century, fishermen's sweaters knitted solely with coarser overhair were replaced by sweaters knitted with a softer, lighter yarn, *samfingið tógv*, a blend of fine inner wool and overhair. People also began to knit lighter types of sweaters for sale, with and without patterns.

The working classes "knitted for a third." This means that they received wool, prepared it, and knitted stockings or sweaters in return for a third of their final sale value. They would hand the pieces over to their local store, and receive their payment in the form of an exchange for household goods adding up to the correct total. This was common all the way up to 1980.

In addition to stockings and sweaters, the Faroese have traditionally knitted hats, mittens, *skóleistar* (slippers), and a distinctive triangular shawl. Knitting and knitting culture remain deeply rooted in the Faroe Islands, and most Faroese women still know how to knit.

BASIC KNITTING TIPS

We tried to design all the patterns in this book so there would be something for every taste and for various levels of experience. We've also tried to describe the process of crafting every single garment as clearly as possible in every single pattern. There are techniques we assume anyone choosing to pick up this book will know—for example, we don't explain in detail how to finish a sweater or cardigan. If you're an experienced knitter, you probably have your own favorite methods of doing things and, of course, you can work as you please. If you're less experienced, we've tried to gather a few general tips and tricks in this section. Sometimes it's easier to see techniques demonstrated than to have them explained, and you'll find many helpful instruction videos on the internet. Search the net if you're uncertain!

READ THROUGH THE ENTIRE PATTERN FIRST

Here's the first general rule: Read through the entire pattern before you start knitting! That way, you'll get an overview of the process. Sometimes there are several instructions that need to be followed simultaneously in the pattern, and it's good to be aware of these areas before you get too far into the knitting.

GAUGE

Gauge is listed in every pattern. For a garment to have the correct measurements, it is important to follow the gauge. As a rule, it is useful to knit a gauge swatch, particularly when you don't have prior experience with the yarn you're using. Some people also knit more tightly in pattern than in single-color stockinette knitting. In that case, we recommend that you try a needle that's a U.S. size / metric half size larger when knitting in a color pattern. In some patterns, the gauge is also listed for the length (the number of rows). This measurement is especially important when you are working a raglan shaping or a sweater with a round yoke.

SHORT ROWS

For some of the designs, you'll knit short rows/turns. Short rows are used to lengthen only certain parts of the garment, such as on the sweater Rakul (which is longer in the back than the front), or the cardigans Maria Christina or the Tailor (where this technique is used to make the collar wider at the back neck). Short rows can also be used, for example, to avoid making the front edge too tight in relation to the facing edge, as in the design Anna Kathrina Súsanna. There are different methods for making short rows to avoid holes when the work is turned. Look on the internet for videos that show this—search for "short rows" or "w&t" ("wrap and turn").

BUTTONHOLES

There are several techniques for working knitted buttonholes; try them out until you find a method you like. In the patterns here, we recommend that you bind off 2 stitches on the buttonhole row and then cast on 2 new stitches over the gap on the following row. This is a very simple method that works well with the yarns we use in this book. If you have an extra heavy or extra fine yarn, you might need to use an alternate method. Try out different options! If you're knitting with really heavy yarn, you can try knitting two stitches together followed by a yarnover (as for a lace eyelet). If you want to make more elaborate buttonholes reinforced at the sides, you'll find several methods, as for doubled front bands. Once again, instructional videos on the web can offer good advice.

PICKING UP AND KNITTING STITCHES

In several of the patterns, you'll pick up and knit stitches along the edge of the knitted fabric—for example, along a neck edge or along the front edges. Some of the patterns list approximately how many stitches you need to pick for every 2 inches / 5 centimeters, or the total number to pick up around the neck or something similar. For stockinette, you should, as a general rule, pick up and knit 3 stitches for every 4 rows, but, you should sample first to be sure of the exact ratio. You should avoid holes around the neck, for example—our tip would be to knit two together at those places on the first round where you have too many stitches. Begin on the right side and pick up stitches inside the edge stitch or inside the seam if you have reinforced and cut open a steek. Make sure you follow the same stitch line all the way up when picking up and knitting along a straight edge. If it makes it easier, feel free to use a crochet hook to pick up the stitches.

WORKING BACK AND FORTH OR MAKING A STEEK?

For most of the patterns in this book, we suggest you set up a steek at the center front and for the armholes so you can continue knitting in the round with the right side always facing. A steek is a set of extra stitches that are later reinforced (usually with machine stitching) and then cut open at the center. Some knitters prefer working back and forth to avoid sewing and cutting the knitted fabric. Some knitters are fine with working in pattern on the wrong side while others prefer using the sewing machine to finish. You can, of course, choose to work in a way other than that suggested in the pattern if you prefer!

STEEKING

First and foremost, keep in mind that steek stitches are not included in the stitch count. Steek stitches are added so you have fabric to cut into. In our patterns, the steek is usually 3 or 4 stitches wide, depending on the thickness of the yarn and whether you're working in a single color. Some knitters work steek stitches in a contrast color (perhaps with one stitch shifting on the next row, as in check pattern). If you use that method, you'll avoid sewing over long yarn floats on the back of the work. Some knitters prefer knitting all steek stitches, while others purl the outermost stitches because they'll lie more smoothly on the inside. Try each of these methods and choose the one that works best for you.

BIND OFF OR SET ASIDE STITCHES?

Usually, for the patterns in this book, you will bind off for the neck and shoulders and then join the garment pieces in finishing. It can be easiest to do this as you proceed. However, you might prefer to place the stitches on a holder and then join the seams with Kitchener stitch when finishing. This method of finishing can be a good alternative because you avoid having little "hard" edges on the wrong side of the garment—particularly when you're using very heavy yarn. Knitting the stitches together with three-needle bind-off is another good option.

REINFORCING AND CUTTING STEEKS

This is without a doubt the scariest part of finishing! In order to make sure the stitches won't unravel, we recommend you sew at least two stitch lines, with both straight and zigzag stitches, on each side of the center steek stitch. Check the wrong side before cutting to make sure everything is smooth and well-reinforced. Carefully cut up the center stitch, between the stitching lines.

ATTACHING SLEEVES

There are several methods you can use for attaching sleeves. You can, for example, choose to use machine stitching to attach the sleeves to the body with the right sides facing; or you can sew from the wrong side using back stitch. Keep in mind that there are always more rows in length than there are stitches in width per 4 inches / 10 centimeters. You must evenly space skipped rows on the armhole side, as when you pick up and knit stitches along an edge. (See "Picking up and Knitting Stitches," on the previous page, which suggests picking up 3 sts for every 4 rows). Count before you start to sew to ensure the stitches are as evenly spaced as possible all around the armhole.

FACINGS

Both because it will look well-finished and to protect the cut edges against unnecessary wear, we recommend that you knit facings to cover any raw edges. You have a lot of options! A facing can be knitted as a part of the front bands and neck and then folded double, or it can be made at the top of a sleeve so as to lie on the inside and cover any raw edges. You can also pick up and knit stitches for a facing, just as for working front bands (see page 5). If you're holding two strands of yarn together for the garment, as for some of the patterns in this book, it's best to knit the facing with only a single strand to avoid unnecessary thickness and clumping. Make sure you pick up and knit stitches so they aren't visible on the right side. The facing will be finest if you work in stockinette, making sure to work so the wrong (purl) side will face in when you turn the facing to cover any raw edges. Once again, you'll find helpful pictures and videos on the internet for various styles of facings.

ABBREVIATIONS

BO	bind off (= British cast off)
cm	centimeter(s)
CO	cast on
est	established
g	gram(s)
in	inch(es)
k	knit
k2tog	knit 2 together = 1 stitch decreased; right-leaning decrease
m	meter(s)
M1	make 1 = lift strand between two sts and knit into back loop
p	purl
pm	place marker
psso	pass slipped st over
rnd(s)	round(s)
RS	right side
sl m	slip marker
ssk	(sl 1 st knitwise) 2 times; knit the stitches together through back loops = 1 stitch decreased; left-leaning decrease
st(s)	stitch(es)
tog	together
WS	wrong side
yd(s)	yard(s)
yo	yarnover

Good luck!

FISHERMAN'S SWEATER MOTIFS

The Faroese fisherman's sweater *bátsmanstroyggja*, literally a "boatman's sweater," is also known as a *skipstroyggja*, a "ship sweater," and is knitted in *samfingið* yarn, which is a blend of fine inner wool and coarse overhair. The long straight overhair and lanolin in the wool make the sweater water repellent. *Bátsmanstroyggja* motifs all have individual names, and include minute pattern repeats with short floats on the wrong side. Fisherman's sweaters are usually patterned all over and knitted in two or three colors, which makes them particularly insulating. Warm and sturdy, they bear up wonderfully against the North Atlantic weather.

FISHERMAN'S SWEATER

A classic fisherman's sweater, knitted in heavy Norwegian wool to emulate the Faroese *bátmanstroyggja* as closely as possible. It's loose-fitting and can be made for both men and women. The body is knitted in the round with drop-shoulder sleeves, which was and still is characteristic of Faroese sweaters. The pattern motif is called *stóraskák og teinur*—"large streak and bar"—and is knitted in two colors. In addition to the motif described in the instructions here, there are five other motifs with the same number of stitches in the repeat that could easily be substituted or combined. All six motifs are illustrated in this book.

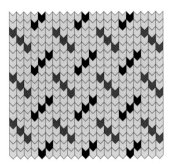

Large streak and bar

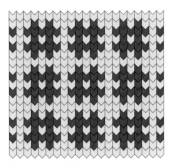

Large streak back and forth

Tines

14

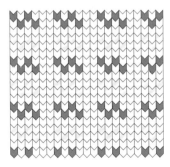

Double streak

Grandmother's touch

Shanks

"When I was young, we knitted sweaters for sale every day. My sister and I would both knit the body of the same sweater at the same time. We would sit across from each other with the body between us and knit with 10-12 knitting needles, which our father had made out of bamboo. One day, Father was so tired of seeing us knit the same motif, the large streak and bar, that he drew another one for us."

Fridrikka, age 90

Sizes
XS (S, M, L, XL, XXL)

Finished Measurements
Chest: 36¼ (39½, 42½, 45¾, 48¾, 52) in / 92 (100, 108, 116, 124, 132) cm
Length: 26 (26¾, 27½, 28¼, 29¼, 30) in / 66 (68, 70, 72, 74, 76) cm
Sleeve length: 19¼ (19¾, 20½, 21, 21¼, 21¾) in / 49 (50, 52, 53, 54, 55) cm or desired length.
All measurements refer to the finished garment sizing and are calculated with the listed gauge.

Materials
Yarn: CYCA #5 (Bulky) Sandnes Garn Fritidsgarn (100% Norwegian wool, 77 yd/70 m / 50 g)

Color Suggestions:
Color 1: Natural Heather 2641
Color 2: Brown 3082
Color 3: Dark Brown Heather 4071

Yarn Amounts:
Color 1: 550 (600, 650, 700, 750, 800) g
Color 2: 100 (150, 150, 150, 200, 200) g
Color 3: 100 (150, 150, 150, 200, 200) g

Needles
U.S. sizes 8 and 9 / 5 and 5.5 mm: Circulars and sets of 5 dpn

Gauge
15 sts in stockinette on larger needles = 4 in / 10 cm
Adjust needle sizes to obtain correct gauge if necessary.

Front and Back
With Color 1 and smaller circular, CO 128 (140, 152, 164, 176, 188) sts. Join, being careful not to twist cast-on row. Pm for beginning of rnd. Work around in k2, p2 ribbing for 2½ in / 6 cm for all sizes. Change to larger circular and knit 1 rnd, increasing 10 sts evenly spaced around = 138 (150, 162, 174, 186, 198) sts. Pm at each side with 69 (75, 81, 87, 93, 99) sts each for front and back. Knit around in Pattern A, beginning at the arrow for chosen size, until body measures 24¾ (25½, 26½, 27¼, 27½, 28¼) in / 63 (65, 67, 69, 70, 72) cm.

BO the center front 17 (19, 19, 21, 21, 23) sts for the neck. Work to the beginning of the rnd and cut yarn. Begin again at the neck at the right side. Working back and forth in stockinette and charted pattern as est, shape neck by binding off, on every row, 4,2 (4,2; 4,2; 4,2; 4,2,1; 4,2,1) sts at neck edge. *At the same time*, when piece is approx. ⅜ in / 1 cm shorter than total length, BO the center back 27 (29, 29, 31, 33, 35) sts for back neck. Work each side separately. Continue, binding off 1 st at neck edge once for all sizes = 20 (22, 25, 27, 29, 31) sts rem for each shoulder. Continue in stockinette and pattern until piece reaches total finished length. BO on either the 3rd or 6th pattern row for the most pleasing look. Work the opposite of back neck the same way, reversing shaping to match.

Sleeves
With Color 1 and smaller dpn, CO 32 (32, 36, 40, 40, 44) sts. Divide sts onto dpn. Join, being careful not to twist cast-on row. Pm for beginning of rnd. Work around in k2, p2 ribbing for 2½ in / 6 cm for all sizes. Change to larger dpn and knit 1 rnd, increasing 1 st. Knit around in Pattern A: Note the arrow at the center of the pattern, and count out the stitches so you can center the pattern. Shape sleeve by increasing as follows every 1 (1, 1, 1¼, 1¼) in / 2½ (2½, 2½, 3, 3, 3) cm: K1, M1, knit until 1 st rem, M1, k1). Increase a total of 18 (19,

19, 18, 19, 18) times = 69 (71, 75, 77, 79, 81) sts. Continue in pattern without further shaping until sleeve reaches finished measurement for your size or desired length. Finish on a Rnd 3 or 6 for the most pleasing look. Knit 1 rnd with Color 1 or the last rnd of pattern. Turn the sleeve inside out and work 3 rows back and forth in stockinette for the facing. Loosely BO knitwise on the 4th row. Make the second sleeve the same way.

Finishing
Gently steam press the garment. Measure and mark the depth of armhole to match the width across top of sleeve. Machine stitch armholes on each side of the center stitch at each side (see page 5). Carefully cut open armholes. Seam shoulders.

Neckband
With Color 1 and smaller circular, pick up and knit about 64 (64, 68, 72, 76, 76) sts around the neck. The stitch count must be a multiple of 4. Work around in k2, p2 ribbing for approx. 5½ in / 14 cm. BO loosely in ribbing. Fold the neckband to the RS.

Attach Sleeves
Pin each sleeve around armhole centered at the shoulder seam and underarm. Beginning at the shoulder, sew each side separately, sewing inside the facing.

Sew the facing down over the cut edges on the WS of each sleeve.
Weave in all ends neatly on WS.

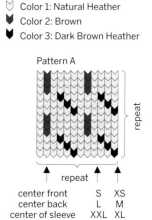

Color 1: Natural Heather
Color 2: Brown
Color 3: Dark Brown Heather

Pattern A

repeat

repeat

center front   S   XS
center back   L   M
center of sleeve   XXL   XL

SIGRID

A long jacket inspired by traditional fishermen's sweaters and knitted in heavy Norwegian wool yarn. The jacket has hidden closures at the front, a high collar, and pockets. Several of the *bátsmanstroyggja* motifs are named for their place of origin. The motif used here is called *Jógvansstovumynstrið*, which means "Jógvan's house motif."

Sizes
S (M, L, XL)

Finished Measurements
Chest: 39¾ (43, 46, 49¼) in / 101 (109, 117, 125) cm
Length: 35 (36¼, 37½, 38¼) in / 89 (92, 95, 97) cm
Sleeve length: 22 (22¾, 23¾, 24) in / 56 (58, 60, 61) cm or desired length.
All measurements refer to the finished garment sizing and are calculated with the listed gauge.

Materials
Yarn: CYCA #5 (Bulky) Sandnes Garn Fritidsgarn (100% Norwegian wool, 77 yd/70 m / 50 g)

Color Suggestions:
Color 1: Navy Blue 5575
Color 2: Natural Heather 2641

Yarn Amounts:
Color 1: 650 (700, 750, 800) g
Color 2: 250 (300, 350, 400) g

Notions
7 large press buttons

Needles
U.S. sizes 8 and 9 / 5 and 5.5 mm: Circulars and sets of 5 dpn

Gauge
15 sts in stockinette on larger needles = 4 in / 10 cm
Adjust needle sizes to obtain correct gauge if necessary.

Front and Back
With Color 1 and smaller circular, CO 148 (160, 172, 184) sts. Work back and forth as follows:
Row 1 (WS): K1 (edge st), (p2, k2) to last 3 sts, end with p2, k1 (edge st).
Row 2 (RS): K1 (edge st), (k2, p2) to last 3 sts, end with k2, k1 (edge st).
Rep Rows 1-2 (with the outermost st at each side always knitted), until ribbing measures 7 in / 18 cm. End with a RS row. Next, knit 3 rows = 2 garter ridges and, *on the 1st row*, decrease 4 sts evenly spaced across = 144 (156, 168, 180) sts rem. It will look best if you decrease on a WS row; in this case, a knit row on the WS.

Pm at center back = the middle of the back with 72 (78, 84, 90) sts on each side of the marker. Now the jacket will be worked in the round. Change to larger circular and join; pm at beginning of rnd. CO 3 sts at the end of the round (= center front steek sts to be reinforced and cut later; see page 5). Do not work the steek sts in pattern and note that the steek sts are not included in any stitch counts. Work in stockinette and Pattern A in the round. Begin at the bottom right of the chart and work the repeat over the first 72 (78, 84, 90) sts = to center back of jacket. Continue the repeat after the arrow on the chart over the last 72 (78, 84, 90) sts.

Continue around in charted pattern until the piece measures 11¾ (12¾, 13½, 14¼) in / 30 (32, 34, 36) cm. Now use two strands of a smooth contrast-color waste yarn to mark the pockets. Knit the first 7 (8, 9, 11) sts in pattern, knit the next 20 (21, 22, 21) sts with a strand of waste yarn. Slide the sts with waste yarn back to the left needle and knit them with colors 1 and 2 in pattern.
Knit until 27 (29, 31, 32) sts rem and knit the next 20 (21, 22, 21) sts with waste yarn. Slide the sts with waste yarn back to the left needle and knit them with Colors 1 and 2 in pattern;

knit the last st of rnd.
Continue around in pattern until the front measures 31½ (32¼, 33½, 34¼) in / (80 (82, 85, 87) cm. BO the 3 steek sts + 5 (5, 5, 5) sts on each side of steek for the neck. Continue in pattern, working back and forth. At neck edge at each side, at the beginning of every row, BO 3,1,1,1,1; (3,2,1,1,1; 3,2,1,1,1; 3,2,2,1,1) sts. *At the same time*, when the piece is about ¾ in / 2 cm shorter than total length, BO the center 30 (32, 32, 34) sts for back neck. Work each side separately. Continue by also decreasing 1 st at back neck for all sizes once = 44 (48, 54, 58) sts rem. When piece is total length, BO. Work the other side the same way, reversing shaping to match.

Sleeves
With Color 1 and smaller dpn, CO 32 (32, 36, 36) sts. Divide sts onto dpn. Join, being careful not to twist cast-on row. Pm for beginning of rnd. Work around in k2, p2 ribbing for 4 in / 10 cm for all sizes. Purl 1 rnd and, *at the same time*, increase 8 (10, 8, 10) sts evenly spaced around = 40 (42, 44, 46) sts. Increasing on a purl rnd makes for a smoother overall look. Now knit 1 rnd, purl 1 rnd = 2 garter ridges. Change to larger dpn. Knit around in Pattern A: Note the arrow at the center of the pattern, and count out the stitches so you can center the pattern. Shape sleeve by increasing as follows every ¾ in / 2 cm: K1, M1, knit until 1 st rem, M1, k1. Increase a total of 17 (18, 19, 19) times = 74 (78, 82, 84) sts. Continue in pattern without further shaping until sleeve reaches finished measurement for your size or desired length. Turn the sleeve inside out and work 4 rows back and forth in stockinette for the facing. Loosely BO knitwise on the 5th row. Make the second sleeve the same way.

Finishing

Gently steam press the garment. Machine stitch on each side of the 3 steek sts at center front (see page 5). Carefully cut open at center of steek.

Machine stitch armholes on each side of the center stitch at each side (see page 5). Carefully cut open armholes. Seam shoulders.

Collar

With Color 1 and smaller circular, pick up and knit 58 (62, 66, 70) sts around the neck. The stitch count should be a multiple of 2, so adjust the count as necessary. Work back and forth in k1, p1 ribbing for ¾ in / 2 cm. Now increase 10 sts evenly spaced across = 68 (72, 76, 80) sts. The stitch count should be a multiple of 4, so adjust the count as necessary. Work back and forth in k2, p2 ribbing + 1 edge st at each side. On the first row, adjust the stitch count so that the row begins and ends with k2 + 1 edge st as seen on the RS. Continue in ribbing until collar measures approx. 14¼ in / 36 cm. BO loosely in ribbing.

Left Front Band

With Color 1 and smaller circular, beginning at the top of the collar, pick up and knit approx. 172 (176, 180, 184) sts along the collar and down the left front edge. The stitch count must be a multiple of 4. Work back and forth as follows:
Row 1 (WS): K1 (edge st), (p2, k2) until 3 sts rem and end with p2, k1 (edge st).
Row 2 (RS): K1 (edge st), (k2, p2) until 3 sts rem and end with k2, k1 (edge st). Rep Rows 1-2 (keeping the outermost st at each side as an edge st that is always knitted), until the ribbing measures approx. 2 in / 5 cm. BO loosely in ribbing.

Right Front

Work as for left front, but begin at the lower edge of the right front.

Fold the collar in half towards the WS

and sew it down smoothly on WS. Sew the front bands along the collar so they are doubled.

Facings over Cut Edges

If desired, you can pick up and knit sts for a facing over the cut edges on the inside along the front bands. Pick up and knit approx. 15 sts for every 4 in / 10 cm. Work 3 rows back and forth in stockinette and then BO. Sew the facings over the cut edges.

Pockets

Insert a smaller dpn into the sts below the waste yarn and another dpn into the sts above the waste yarn. Carefully remove waste yarn. Divide the sts onto 4 dpn, picking up and knitting 1 extra st at each side to avoid holes. With Color 1, work the first 2 rows as follows:
Rnd 1: Knit all sts.
Rnd 2: Purl the sts from the lower edge (= 1 ridge at front) and knit the rem sts.

Now continue around in stockinette for approx. 6 in / 15 cm. BO. Sew the pockets down at lower edge.

Attach Sleeves

Pin each sleeve around armhole centered at the shoulder seam and underarm. Beginning at the shoulder, sew each side separately, sewing inside the facing.

Sew the facing down over the cut edges on the WS of each sleeve.

Sew on the press buttons, with the top one about 3½ in / 9 cm down from the top of the neck edge and the bottom one about 5¼ in / 13 cm from the cast-on row.

Weave in all ends neatly on WS.

Color 1: Navy Blue
Color 2: Natural Heather

Pattern A

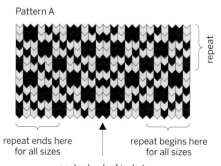

repeat

repeat ends here for all sizes

repeat begins here for all sizes

center back of jacket
center of sleeve

SEVEN STARS

A long feminine take on the classic fisherman's sweater. The turtleneck and cuffs are wide and chunky, cozily knitted with soft alpaca-wool and silk-mohair yarns. The motif is called *sjeystjørna*—the Faroese name for the Pleiades or "Seven Sisters" star constellation—probably because it's made up of seven small stars set in a rhomboid pattern.

Sizes
XS-S (M, L-XL)

Finished Measurements
Chest: 34¾ (41¼, 48½) in / 88 (105, 123) cm
Length: 34¼ (35½, 36¾) in / 87 (90, 93) cm
Sleeve length: 22¾ (23¾, 24½) in / 58 (60, 62) cm or desired length.
All measurements refer to the finished garment sizing and are calculated with the listed gauge.

Materials
Yarn:
CYCA #4 (worsted, afghan, Aran)
Sandnes Garn Alpakka Ull (65% alpaca, 35% wool, 109 yd/100 m / 50 g)
CYCA #4 (worsted, afghan, Aran)
Sandnes Garn Silk Mohair (60% kid mohair, 25% silk, 15% wool, 306 yd/280 m / 50 g)

Color Suggestions:
Color 1: Alpakka ull: Dark Gray Heather 1053 + Silk Mohair: Gray 1076
Color 2: Alpakka ull: Charcoal Heather 1088 + Silk Mohair: Black 1099
Color 3: Alpakka ull: Gray Heather 1042 + Silk Mohair: Gray 1076

Yarn Amounts:
Color 1: Alpakka ull: 550 (600, 650) g + Silk Mohair: 200 (200, 250) g
Color 2: Alpakka ull: 100 (150, 200) g + Silk Mohair: 50 (100, 100) g
Color 3: Alpakka ull: 50 (50, 50) g + Silk Mohair: small amounts of Color 1

Needles
U.S. sizes 8 and 10 / 5 and 6 mm: Circulars and sets of 5 dpn

Gauge
16 sts in stockinette on larger needles = 4 in / 10 cm
Adjust needle sizes to obtain correct gauge if necessary.

Front and Back
With Color 1 (= 1 strand of each yarn held together) and smaller circular, CO 140 (168, 196) sts. Join, being careful not to twist cast-on row; pm for beginning of rnd. Work around in k2, p2 ribbing until piece measures 7 in / 18 cm. Pm at each side with 71 (85, 99) sts for the front and 69 (83, 97) sts for the back. Change to larger circular and work around in stockinette and Pattern A until piece measures approx. 21¾ (22¾, 24) in / 55 (58, 61) cm. Now work Pattern B in the round. When piece measures 25¼ (26, 26¾) in / 64 (66, 68) cm, shape armholes at each side: BO 4 sts on each side of each side marker = 8 sts bound off at each side. CO 4 new sts over each gap = steeks (see page 5). Work the steek sts in a single color; they are not included in any stitch counts. Continue in Pattern B as est and, *at the same time*, on every other round, at the armholes, on each side of the 4 steek sts, BO 2,1 (2,1,1; 2,1,1,1) sts. Continue without further shaping until until piece measures 32¼ (33½, 34¾) in / 82 (85, 88) cm. BO the center front 15 (17, 19) sts for the neck. Work up to the beginning of the rnd and cut yarn. Begin at the center front and work back and forth in stockinette and pattern as est. Shape neck by binding off at each side: at the beginning of every row 2,2,1 (2,2,2; 2,2,2) sts. When work is about ⅜-¾ in / 1-2 cm shorter than total length, BO the center back 21 (25, 27) sts for back neck. Work each side separately. Decrease 1 st at back neck once = 16 (20, 25) sts rem for shoulder. Continue in pattern until piece reaches total length and then BO. Work the other side the same way, reversing shaping to match.

Sleeves
With Color 1 (= 1 strand of each yarn held together) and smaller dpn, CO 36 (40, 44) sts. Divide sts onto dpn. Join and pm for beginning of rnd. Work around in k2, p2 ribbing for 6¼ in / 16 cm.
Change to larger dpn. Knit 1 rnd, increasing 6 (4, 2) sts evenly spaced around = 42 (44, 46) sts.
Shape Sleeve by increasing as follows: every 1 in / 2.5 cm (all sizes): K1, M1, knit until 1 st rem, M1, k1. Increase a total of 15 (16, 17) times = 72 (76, 80) sts. Continue without further shaping until sleeve reaches finished measurement for your size or desired length. BO 4 sts at the end and then the beginning of the next rnd = 8 sts decreased at underarm. Continue back and forth in stockinette, binding off 2,1 (2,1,1; 2,1,1,1) sts on each side at the beginning of the row.
Turn the sleeve inside out and work 3 rows back and forth in stockinette for the facing. Loosely BO knitwise on the 4th row. Make the second sleeve the same way.

Finishing
Gently steam press the garment. Machine stitch armholes on each side of the center stitch at each side (see page 5). Carefully cut open armholes. Seam shoulders.

Neckband
With Color 1 (= 1 strand of each yarn held together) and smaller circular, pick up and knit approx. 72 (76, 80) sts around the neck = Row 1 on RS. The stitch count must be a multiple of 4. Join; pm for beginning of rnd. Work around in k2, p2 ribbing for 1¼ in / 3 cm. Change to larger circular and continue in k2, p2 ribbing until neckband is approx. 13¾ in / 35 cm long. BO loosely in ribbing. Fold neckband forward.

Attach Sleeves
Pin each sleeve around armhole centered at the shoulder seam and underarm. Beginning at the shoulder, sew each side separately, sewing inside the facing.

Sew the facing down over the cut
edges on the WS of each sleeve.

Weave in all ends neatly on WS.

Pattern B

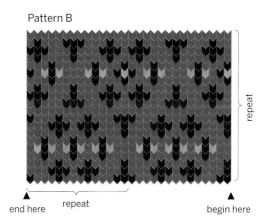

end here   repeat   begin here

               repeat

Pattern A

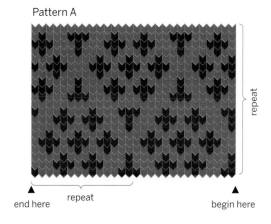

end here   repeat   begin here

               repeat

Color 1: Dark Gray Heather + Gray
Color 2: Charcoal Heather + Black
Color 3: Gray Heather + Gray

35

INGIBJØRG

A short, feminine variation on the
fisherman's sweater, knitted in a blend of
soft alpaca and silk-mohair. The shoulders
are accentuated by seed stitching on top
and a slim rolled edge. The motif is called
klíputongin, which means "the pincer."

Sizes
S (M, L, XL)

Finished Measurements
Chest: 33½ (36¾, 40¼, 43¾) in / 85 (93, 102, 111) cm
Length: 21¾ (22½, 23¼, 24) in / 55 (57, 59, 61) cm
Sleeve length: 18½ (19, 19¼, 19¾) in / 47 (48, 49, 50) cm or desired length.
All measurements refer to the finished garment sizing and are calculated with the listed gauge.

Materials
Yarn:
CYCA #1 (fingering) Sandnes Garn Mini Alpakka (100% alpaca, 164 yd/150 m / 50 g)
CYCA #4 (worsted, afghan, Aran) Sandnes Garn Silk Mohair (60% kid mohair, 25% silk, 15% wool, 306 yd/280 m / 50 g)

Color Suggestions:
Color 1: Mini Alpakka: Natural 1012 + Silk Mohair: Natural 1012
Color 2: Mini Alpakka: Charcoal Heather 1088 + Silk Mohair: Black 1099
Color 3: Silk Mohair: Black 1099

Yarn Amounts:
Color 1: Mini Alpakka: 300 (350, 400, 450) g + Silk Mohair: 100 (100, 100, 150) g
Color 2: Mini Alpakka: 100 (100, 100, 100) g + Silk Mohair: 50 (50, 50, 50) g
Color 3: Silk Mohair: small amounts

Needles
U.S. sizes 6 and 9 / 4 and 5.5 mm: Circulars and sets of 5 dpn;
U.S. size 2.5 / 3 mm for tucks at shoulders

Gauge
18 sts in stockinette on U.S. 9 / 5.5 mm needles = 4 in / 10 cm
Adjust needle sizes to obtain correct gauge if necessary.

NOTE: If you knit single color stockinette more loosely than two-color pattern knitting, use needles one U.S. or one-half metric size smaller when working in stockinette.

Seed Stitch
Row 1: (K1, p1) across.
Row 2 and all subsequent rows: Work purl over knit and knit over purl.

Front and Back
With Color 1 (= 1 strand of each yarn held together) and U.S. 6 / 4 mm circular, CO 152 (168, 184, 200) sts. Join, being careful not to twist cast-on row; pm for beginning of rnd. Work around in k2, p2 ribbing until piece measures 2½ in / 6 cm. Pm at each side with 76 (84, 92, 100) sts each for front and back. Change to U.S. 9 / 5.5 mm circular and work around in stockinette and Pattern A. Begin and end at each side marker as shown on the chart. Make sure that the pattern does *not* become symmetrical between the side markers—this will be adjusted when the body is divided for front and back. Work in pattern as est until body measures 14¼ (14½, 15, 15½) in / 36 (37, 38, 39) cm. Now BO 5 sts after each marker and 2 sts before each marker at each side = 7 sts decreased, centered over the stripes at each side of the body. Work front and back separately.

Back
Work back and forth in Pattern A as est and, *at the same time,* shape armholes at each side: at the beginning of every row at each side, BO 2,2,1,1 (2,2,1,1; 2,2,1,1,1; 2,2,1,1,1) sts = 57 (65, 71, 79) sts rem. Continue without further shaping until piece measures approx. 20 (21, 21¾, 22½) in / 51 (53, 55, 57) cm. It will look best if you end on either a complete or half pattern repeat. BO all sts.

Front
Work back and forth in Pattern A as est and, *at the same time,* shape armholes as for back. Continue without further shaping until piece measures approx. 19¼ (20, 21, 21¾) in / 49 (51, 53, 55) cm. BO the center 25 (31, 35, 41) sts for the front neck. Work each side separately. At neck edge, BO 1,1 sts = 14 (15, 16, 17) sts remain for each shoulder. Continue in pattern until front is same length as back. BO at the same pattern row as for back. Work the opposite side of neck the same way, reversing shaping to match.

Sleeves
With Color 1 (= 1 strand of each yarn held together) and U.S. 6 / 4 mm dpn, CO 40 (44, 44, 48) sts. Divide sts onto dpn. Join and pm for beginning of rnd. Work around in k2, p2 ribbing for 2½ in / 6 cm.
Change to U.S. 9 / 5.5 mm dpn and work around in stockinette.
Shape Sleeve by increasing as follows every 1¾ (1¾, 1¼-1½, 1½) in / 4.5 (4.5, 3.5-4, 4) cm: K1, M1, knit until 1 st rem, M1, k1). Increase a total of 9 (9, 11, 11) times = 58 (62, 66, 70) sts. Continue without further shaping until sleeve reaches finished measurement for your size or desired length to underarm.
Sleeve Cap: BO 4 sts each at the end of rnd and beginning of next rnd = 8 sts decreased at underarm. Continue back and forth in stockinette, binding off 2 sts twice at beginning of row on each side of underarm. Next, decrease 1 st at the beginning of each row until 24 sts rem for all sizes. Now BO 2 sts at the beginning of every row 2 times on each side = 16 sts rem for the shoulder on all sizes. Work in seed stitch over these 16 sts for approx. 3 (3¼, 3½, 3¾) in / 8 (8.5, 9, 9.5) cm or until the section is as long as the width of the shoulder on the front. BO all sts. Make the second sleeve the same way.

Finishing
Gently steam press the garment.
Attach Sleeves: Beginning at the neck on the shoulder, sew sleeve to the body along the edge of the seed section at the top of the sleeve. Sew each side separately.

42

Tuck at Shoulder

With Color 3 and U.S. size 2.5 / 3 mm
needles, pick up and knit along the
shoulder seam line. Work back and
forth in stockinette, with the knit side
on the inside and the purl stitches
on the outside. When tuck measures
approx. ⅜-⅝ in / 1-1.5 cm, BO. Make a
tuck at each shoulder seam (4 total).
The tuck will roll inwards. Sew the
short ends to the edges of the front/
back. Seam shoulders.

Collar

With Color 1 (= 1 strand of each yarn
held together) and U.S. 6 / 4 mm
needles, pick up and knit approx. 104
(108, 108, 112) sts around the neck. The
stitch count must be a multiple of 4.
Work around in k2, p2 ribbing for 4¼
in / 11 cm. Change to needles U.S. 9 /
5.5 mm and continue in k2, p2 ribbing
until collar is approx. 9¾ in / 25 cm
long total. BO in ribbing. Roll collar
forward.

Weave in all ends neatly on WS.

43

Pattern A

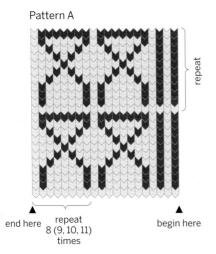

end here   repeat   begin here
8 (9, 10, 11)
times

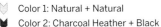
Color 1: Natural + Natural
Color 2: Charcoal Heather + Black

POULA

A soft hat with long black braids, knitted
in a blend of alpaca-wool and silk-mohair.
The motif is called *rossagronin*, which
means "horse's muzzle." Hans Marius
Debes often mentions bonnets in his
stories, and there's something fascinating
about them—we wanted to share a modern
take on these garments. The idea stems
from Tailor Debes' description of wealthy
farmer Poul á Látrinum, who, back in
the day when men wore wigs on solemn
occasions, accessorized his finery with a
braid, fastened to his hair with a black silk
bow.

Sizes
One size

Materials
Yarn:
CYCA #4 (worsted, afghan, Aran)
Sandnes Garn Silk Mohair (60% kid mohair, 25% silk, 15% wool, 306 yd/280 m / 50 g)
CYCA #4 (worsted, afghan, Aran)
Sandnes Garn Alpakka Ull (65% alpaca, 35% wool, 109 yd/100 m / 50 g)

Color Suggestions:
Color 1: Silk Mohair: Black 1099 + Alpakka Ull: Black 1099
Color 2: Alpakka Ull: Putty 1015

Yarn Amounts:
Color 1: Silk Mohair: 50 g + Alpakka Ull: 100 g
Color 2: Alpakka Ull: 50 g

Needles
U.S. size 8 / 5 mm: Circular;
U.S. size 10 / 6 mm: Circular and set of 5 dpn

Gauge
18 sts in stockinette on larger needles = 4 in / 10 cm
Adjust needle sizes to obtain correct gauge if necessary.

With Color 1 (= 1 strand of each yarn held together) and smaller circular, CO 108 sts. Work back and forth in ribbing as follows:
Row 1 (WS): K1 (edge st), (p2, k2) until 3 sts rem; end p2, k1 (edge st).
Row 2 (RS): K1 (edge st), (k2, p2) until 3 sts rem; end k2, k1 (edge st).
Rep Rows 1-2 until ribbing measures approx. 2½ in / 6 cm. End with a WS row. Change to larger circular and continue working back and forth in stockinette and Pattern A. *On the first row*, decrease 4 sts evenly spaced across = 104 sts rem. Work in pattern until piece measures approx. 6¼ in / 16 cm with the last row on the RS. From this point on, the hat is worked in the round. Join and begin by working one stripe with Color 2 (= 1 extra pattern repeat instead of only Color 1) at the center of hat where the pieces meet = 13 stripes in Color 2. Complete the first 24 rnds of Pattern A (= 1 complete repeat).
Pattern A is now repeated *at the same time* as the decreases begin on the next rnd: There will be 1 st less in each color stripe for each decrease rnd. Change to dpn when sts no longer fit around circular.
Decrease Rnd 1: *K2tog at the beginning of each Color 2 stripe = 13 sts decreased. Work 2 rnds without decreasing*. Rep from * to * once more = 78 sts rem.
Decrease Rnd 2: *K2tog at the beginning of each Color 1 stripe = 13 sts decreased. Work 2 rnds without decreasing*. Rep from * to * once more = 52 sts rem.
Decrease Rnd 3: K2tog at the beginning of each Color 2 stripe. Work 2 rnds without decreasing = 39 sts rem.
Decrease Rnd 4: K2tog at the beginning of each Color 1 stripe. Work 2 rnds without decreasing = 26 sts rem.
Decrease Rnd 5: K2tog around = 13 sts rem.
Cut yarn and draw end through rem sts; tighten.

Braids
Braided Cord: With Color 1 (= 1 strand of each yarn held together) and larger circular, CO 60 sts. Work 3 rows back and forth in stockinette. On the last row, BO loosely. Make 2 more cords the same way. Sew the cords to each other, side by side with the knit side out. Sew cords to lower edge of hat along the short ribbed border on one side of the hat. Braid the cords—about 11 in / 28 cm long. Wrap Color 1 yarn around the lower end of the braid.

Make another braid the same way for the other side of the hat.
Weave in all ends neatly on WS.

Color 1: Black + Black
Color 2: Putty

Pattern A

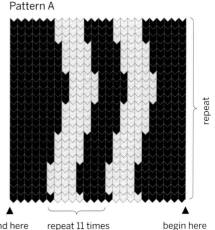

repeat

end here   repeat 11 times   begin here

URD

Urd is a flowing women's sweater with
deep raglan shaping, knitted in soft
alpaca-wool and silk-mohair. The pattern
is a combination of several different
fisherman's motifs, some worked with purl
stitches to add structure to the sweater.

Sizes
XS-S (M, L-XL)

Finished Measurements
Chest: 37¾ (43, 48) in / 96 (109, 122) cm
Length, measured down center front: 28¼ (31½, 34¾) in / 72 (80, 88) cm
Sleeve length: approx. 15 (15¾, 16½) in / 38 (40, 42) cm or desired length.
All measurements refer to the finished garment sizing and are calculated with the listed gauge.

Materials
Yarn:
CYCA #2 (sport, baby) Sandnes Garn Tynn (fine) Alpakka Ull (65% alpaca, 35% wool, 182 yd/166 m / 50 g)
CYCA #4 (worsted, afghan, Aran) Sandnes Garn Silk Mohair (60% kid mohair, 25% silk, 15% wool, 306 yd/280 m / 50 g)

Color Suggestions:
Color 1: Tynn Alpakka Ull: Black 1099 + Silk Mohair: Black 1099
Color 2: Tynn Alpakka Ull: Moss Green 9573 + Silk Mohair: Moss Green 9573
Color 3: Tynn Alpakka Ull: Gray Heather 1042 + Silk Mohair: Natural 1012

Yarn Amounts:
Color 1: Tynn Alpakka Ull: 100 (100, 150) g + Silk Mohair: 50 (50, 50) g
Color 2: Tynn Alpakka Ull: 50 (100, 100) g + Silk Mohair: 50 (50, 50) g
Color 3: Tynn Alpakka Ull: 300 (350, 400) g + Silk Mohair: 150 (150, 200) g

Needles
U.S. sizes 9 and 10 / 5.5 and 6 mm: Circular and set of 5 dpn

Gauge
18 sts and 17 rnds in stockinette on larger needles = 4 in / 10 cm
Adjust needle sizes to obtain correct gauge if necessary.

Front and Back
With Color 1 (= 1 strand each yarn held together) and smaller circular, CO 172 (196, 220) sts. Join, being careful not to twist cast-on row; pm for beginning of rnd. Work around in k1, p1 ribbing for 1½ in / 4 cm. Change to larger circular. Pm at each side with 86 (98, 110) sts each for front and back. Work Pattern A once (= 5 side sts). Work Pattern B, beginning and ending at the arrow for your size. Repeat Pattern A (= the side st on the other side) and Pattern B once more. Continue as est until piece measures 16¼ (17¾, 19) in / 41 (45, 48) cm.
Shape Armholes: BO 7 sts after each marker and 2 sts before each marker = 9 sts bound off at each side = the 5 side sts + 2 sts at each side = 77 (89, 101) sts rem each for back and front. Set body aside while you knit the sleeves.

Please Read Before You Begin Knitting the Sleeves
In order for the patterns on the sleeves and the body to match when all the pieces are knitted together, work as follows:
Measure the length from the point where you ended the body and about 15 (15¾, 16½) in / 38 (49, 42) cm down or measure the desired sleeve length. Now you can calculate where in the pattern you should begin after you've worked the 1½ in / 4 cm in ribbing. The ribbing is included in the sleeve length.

Sleeves
With Color 1 (=1 strand each of yarn held together) and smaller dpn, CO 36 (38, 40) sts. Divide sts onto dpn. Join, being careful not to twist cast-on row; pm for beginning of rnd. Work around in k1, p1 ribbing for 1½ in / 4 cm. Pm in the first st and then in the 19th (20th, 21st) st = 17 (18, 19) sts on each side of the two markers. The center st of Pattern A is the 1st st of the underarm and the center st of Pattern B marks the center of the sleeve. Change to larger dpn. Continue as follows:
Work the last 3 sts of Pattern A, beginning the pattern as you calculated for your size.
Work Pattern B, counting out from the center st to determine where to begin the pattern, and begin on the same rnd in pattern as for Pattern A. When 2 sts rem, work the first 2 sts of Pattern A.
Shape Sleeves: Every ⅝ (⅜-⅝, ⅜) in / 1.5 (1-1.5, 1) cm, increase 1 st with M1 on each side of the 5 sts of Pattern A 21 (26, 30) times = 78 (90, 100) sts. Work the new sts into pattern as well as possible. Continue until sleeve is desired length and end on the same rnd in the patterns as for the body. BO the center st at the center of the underarm and 4 sts on each side of the center st = 9 sts bound-off = 69 (81, 91) sts rem. Set sleeve aside and make another the same way.

Raglan Shaping
Place all of the pieces onto a circular in the correct order and, *at the same time*, knit the first rnd: Knit the last st of the right sleeve tog with the first st of the back = marked st. Work Pattern B as est over the sts of back and knit the last st tog with the first st of left sleeve = marked st. Work Pattern B as est over the sleeve and knit the last st tog with the first st of front = marked st. Continue in Pattern B as est over front and knit the last st tog with first st of right sleeve = marked st. You have now decreased 4 sts around. The marked sts should always be knitted with Color 3. The 2 sts before and after each marked st should also be worked with Color 3. There should now be 288 (336, 380) sts around. The patterns will not match up in the shifts between the body and sleeves. After Pattern B is completed, the rest of the sweater is worked with Color 3.

The rnds now begin at the back and the raglan shaping is worked as follows:

Knit marked st. Slip next st knitwise, k1, psso. Knit until 2 sts rem before next marked st, k2tog, k marked st, sl 1 knitwise, k1, psso. Continue until 2 sts before next marked st. Decrease as before = 8 sts decreased around.

Work 1 rnd without decreasing. On the next rnd, decrease as explained above. Continue, alternating a decrease rnd with a non-decrease rnd a total of 26 (31, 36) times = 80 (88, 92) sts rem. Leave sts on needle.

Neckband

Change to smaller circular or dpn and Color 2 (= 1 strand of each yarn). Work around in k1, p1 ribbing for 1½ in / 4 cm. BO loosely in ribbing.

Finishing

Seam the underarms. Weave in all ends neatly on WS. Gently steam press the sweater.

Color 1: Black + Black
Color 2: Moss Green + Moss Green
Color 3: Gray Heather + Natural
Color 2: Purl st
Color 1: Purl st

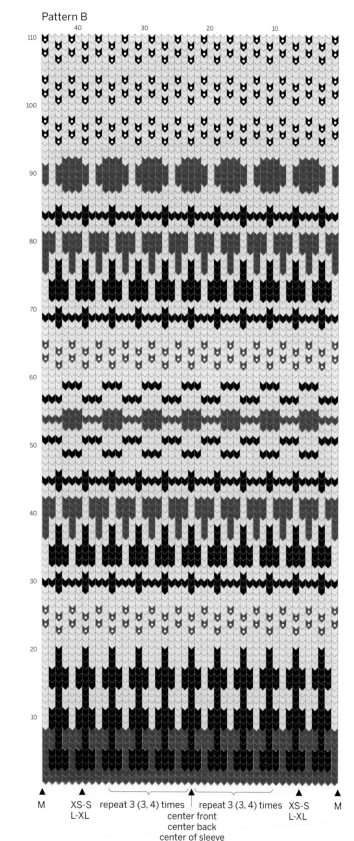

Pattern B

Pattern A

53

M   XS-S   repeat 3 (3, 4) times   repeat 3 (3, 4) times   XS-S   M
     L-XL   L-XL
            center front
            center back
            center of sleeve

center of
underarm

LENA

A long and roomy women's sweater knitted in a very soft blend of alpaca-silk and silk-mohair. The *tímaglasið*, or "hourglass" pattern, embellishes the body and sleeves, while the yoke is knitted in a single color. The pattern was inspired by a story from Tailor Debes about the Tokustova sisters, who lived in the Faroese capital city of Tórshavn and had a special license giving them the right to beg for wool from farmers in outlying areas.

"They were called the Tokustova sisters and they were well known. People in Tokustova were particularly clever. There were four sisters and one brother. He was named Sigvald. Two of the sisters used to travel north to Gjógv every summer. They would stay at my great-grandfather's house. That's why [when Grandmother visited Tórshavn], they wanted to be hospitable to my grandmother, and invited her in. Grandmother said that they were very welcome when they came north to Gjógv. They used to come around the time when the spring wool was washed and dried. And when they came, these city women, they were so fancy and would greet everyone in Danish instead of Faroese, and they showed their passports. They had permission from the bailiff to travel. That was because there were so many people roaming the islands and begging. They would show their papers and give gifts.

As Grandmother used to say, the town ladies were often useful when they came. There weren't any fine needles in the house, and the nearest shop was in Klaksvík. They brought various gifts with them. Some of the town ladies gave two sewing needles with gilded eyes in them, which was such a rarity—gilded eyes! Another gift was a darning needle, and some would offer a triangular needle, and they might also bring little bobbins of white or black sewing thread. And people would give them gifts, too, large bundles of wool. Grandmother said it was special with these sisters from Tokustova, they were so witty and well-dressed, clean and proper. In fact, her mother held them in such high regard that they were allowed to sleep in the bed that was usually reserved for the dean when he visited."

Excerpt from the story "My Grandmother Was in Tórshavn One St. Olaf's Day" in *Tales of the Old Days* by Hans M. Debes, 1977

Sizes
XS-S (M, L-XL)

Finished Measurements
Chest: 42¼ (47¼, 52½) in / 107 (120, 133) cm
Length: 28¾ (30¾, 32¾) in / 73 (78, 83) cm
Sleeve length: 16¼ (16½, 17) in / 41 (42, 43) cm or desired length. All measurements refer to the finished garment sizing and are calculated with the listed gauge.

Materials
Yarn:
CYCA #1 (fingering) Sandnes Garn Alpaca Silk (70% baby alpaca, 30% mulberry silk, 218 yd/199 m / 50 g)
CYCA #4 (worsted, afghan, Aran) Sandnes Garn Silk Mohair (60% kid mohair, 25% silk, 15% wool, 306 yd/280 m / 50 g)

Color Suggestions:
Color 1: Alpaca Silk: Acid Yellow 2005 + Silk Mohair: Acid Yellow 2005
Color 2: Alpaca Silk: White 1002 + Silk Mohair: Natural 1012
Color 3: Alpaca Silk: Charcoal Gray 1088 + Silk Mohair: Black 1099

Yarn Amounts:
Color 1: Alpaca Silk: 50 (50, 50) g + Silk Mohair: 50 (50, 50) g
Color 2: Alpaca Silk: 250 (300, 350) g + Silk Mohair: 150 (200, 200) g
Color 3: Alpaca Silk: 100 (150, 200) g + Silk Mohair: 100 (100, 100) g

Needles
U.S. sizes 6 and 9 / 4 and 5.5 mm: circulars and sets of 5 dpn

Gauge
18 sts in stockinette on larger needles = 4 in / 10 cm
Adjust needle sizes to obtain correct gauge if necessary.

60

NOTE: If you knit single color stockinette more loosely than two-color pattern knitting, use one U.S. or one-half metric smaller needles when working in stockinette.

Front and Back
With Color 1 (= 1 strand each of yarn held together) and smaller circular, CO 192 (216, 240) sts. Join, being careful not to twist cast-on row; pm for beginning of rnd. Work around in garter st, alternating purl and knit rnds (2 rnds = 1 garter ridge) until you've worked 3 ridges. Change to larger circular. Pm at each side with 96 (108, 120) sts each for front and back. Work Pattern A around. Begin and end at each side marker as shown on the chart. Note that the pattern does not match at both sides of the side markers; this will be adjusted when the body is divided for front and back. Continue in pattern until you've completed 7 (8, 9) black "hourglasses" up, including where you will end. Pm at the center of the center hourglass on the front. This marks the place for starting the neck shaping later. Change to Color 1 and continue around in the single color until piece measures 25½ (27½, 29½) in / 65 (70, 75) cm. Find the marker at center front and BO 8 (9, 10) sts on each side of marker = 17 (19, 21) sts bound off for the neck. Now work back and forth. At beginning of every row at neck edge, BO 3,2,2,1,1,1 sts (all sizes). Continue until piece is total length and then BO all sts. There is no bind-off for the back neck.

Sleeves
With Color 1 (= 1 strand each of yarn held together) and smaller dpn, CO 38 (40, 42) sts. Divide sts onto dpn. Join, being careful not to twist cast-on row; pm for beginning of rnd. Work around in garter st, alternating purl and knit rnds (2 rnds = 1 garter ridge) until you've worked 3 ridges. Change to larger dpn.
Continue around in Pattern B and,

on the first rnd, increase 4 (8, 12) sts evenly spaced around = 42 (48 54) sts. To shape the sleeves, begin increasing after the first 14 rnds of Pattern B. You should have 3 black and 4 white stripes centered under the arm and the center black stripe marks the center of underarm. Increase on each side of the outermost white stripes at underarm—there will be 7 sts between the increases. Work the new sts into pattern as well as possible. Increase 1 st as explained above at the beginning and end of the round approx. every ⅝ (⅝-¾, ⅝-¾) in / 1.5 (1.5-2, 1.5-2) cm 21 (20, 19) times = 84 (88, 92) sts. Continue until sleeve is given or desired length. Knit 1 rnd with Color 2 or work the last rnd in pattern. Turn sleeve inside out and work 4 rows back and forth in stockinette for the facing. Loosely BO knitwise. Make the second sleeve the same way.

Finishing
Gently steam press the sweater. Measure and mark the depth of armhole to match the width across top of sleeve. Machine stitch armholes on each side of the center black stripe at each side (see page 5). Carefully cut open armholes. Seam shoulders.

Neckband
With 2 strands of Silk Mohair Color 2 and 1 strand Alpakka Silk Color 2 (= 3 strands held together), and larger circular, pick up and knit approx. 98 (100, 104) sts around neck. The stitch count must be a multiple of 4. Work around in k2, p2 ribbing for 14¼ in / 36 cm. BO in ribbing.

Attach Sleeves
Pin each sleeve around armhole centered at the shoulder seam and underarm. Beginning at the shoulder, sew each side separately, sewing inside the facing.
Sew the facing down over the cut edges on the WS of each sleeve.

Weave in all ends neatly on WS.

Chart A

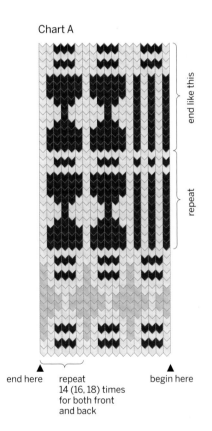

end like this

repeat

Chart B

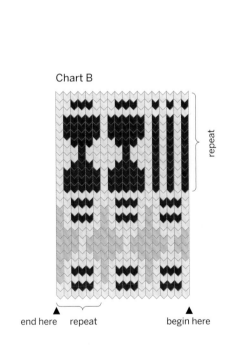

repeat

61

end here   repeat   begin here

end here   repeat   begin here
14 (16, 18) times
for both front
and back

Color 1: Acid Yellow + Acid Yellow
Color 2: White + Natural
Color 3: Charcoal Heather + Black

JACOBINA

A short and roomy women's sweater
knitted in a very soft blend of alpaca-silk
and silk-mohair. The hourglass (*tímaglasið*)
motif is featured on the yoke. Like the Lena
pattern, this sweater was inspired by Tailor
Debes's story about the Tokustova sisters.

"All persons, even the truly impoverished and needy, who for one or another valid reason are unable to earn a living for themselves or their family are hereby strictly prohibited from roaming the islands and begging for wool, regardless of their reason or pretense, unless they have first obtained from their parish priest and the relevant sheriff a certificate attesting to their actual destitution, and forthwith reported to the Bailiff in Tórshavn, who then, pursuant to the special order issued to him, has examined their condition more closely and, unless he comes to their aid in another manner, pursuant to the aforementioned order, has issued them the relevant Begging-Pass, whereby he, owing to the circumstances at hand, entitles them to beg for wool in the provinces."

Royal Decree on General Farming and Bondsmen and Bondswomen in the Faroe Islands, dated May 12, 1777 (known as the Bondage Act, Art. 12, 1777)

Sizes

XS-S (M, L-XL)

Finished Measurements

Chest: 42¼ (47¼, 52½) in / 107 (120, 133) cm

Length: 23¼ (24½, 25½) in / 59 (62, 65) cm

Sleeve length: 16¼ (16½, 17) in / 41 (42, 43) cm or desired length. All measurements refer to the finished garment sizing and are calculated with the listed gauge.

Materials

Yarn:

CYCA #1 (fingering) Sandnes Garn Alpaca Silk (70% baby alpaca, 30% mulberry silk, 218 yd/199 m / 50 g)

CYCA #4 (worsted, afghan, Aran) Sandnes Garn Silk Mohair (60% kid mohair, 25% silk, 15% wool, 306 yd/280 m / 50 g)

Color Suggestions:

Color 1: Alpaca Silk: Charcoal Heather 1088 + Silk Mohair: Black 1099

Color 2: Alpaca Silk: White 1002 + Silk Mohair: Natural 1012

Color 3: Alpaca Silk: Acid Yellow 2005 + Silk Mohair: Acid Yellow 2005

Yarn Amounts:

Color 1: Alpaca Silk: 100 (150, 150) g + Silk Mohair: 100 (100, 150) g

Color 2: Alpaca Silk: 250 (250, 300) g + Silk Mohair: 150 (150, 200) g

Color 3: Alpaca Silk: 50 (50, 50) g + Silk Mohair: 50 (50, 50) g

Needles

U.S. sizes 6 and 9 / 4 and 5.5 mm: circulars and sets of 5 dpn

Gauge

18 sts in stockinette on larger needles = 4 in / 10 cm

Adjust needle sizes to obtain correct gauge if necessary.

NOTE: If you knit single color stockinette more loosely than two-color pattern knitting, use needles one U.S. or one-half metric size smaller when working in stockinette.

Front and Back

With Color 1 (= 1 strand of each yarn held together) and smaller circular, CO 192 (216, 240) sts. Join, being careful not to twist cast-on row; pm for beginning of rnd. Work around in garter st, alternating purl and knit rnds (2 rnds = 1 garter ridge) until you've worked 3 ridges. Change to larger circular. Pm at each side with 96 (108, 120) sts each for front and back. Work around in stockinette until piece measures 14½ (15¾, 17) in / 37 (40, 43) cm. Now work following Pattern A. Pm centered between the two centermost hourglasses on the front. This marker indicates where you will later begin the neck shaping. Continue in pattern until the piece measures 20 (21¼, 22½) in / 51 (54, 57) cm. Find the marker at center front and BO 8 (9, 10) sts on each side of the marker = 17 (19, 21) sts bound-off for neck. Now work back and forth in pattern, and, *at the same time,* at neck edge on every row, BO 3,2,2,1,1,1 sts (all sizes). Continue until pattern is complete and the piece is total length. BO all sts. There is no bind off for the back neck.

Sleeves

With Color 1 (= 1 strand each of yarn held together) and smaller dpn, CO 38 (40, 42) sts. Divide sts onto dpn. Join, being careful not to twist cast-on row; pm for beginning of rnd. Work around in garter st, alternating purl and knit rnds (2 rnds = 1 garter ridge) until you've worked 3 ridges. Change to larger dpn and Color 2.

Continue around in stockinette and, *on the first rnd,* increase 4 (8, 12) sts evenly spaced around = 42 (48, 54) sts. To shape the sleeves, work as follows: approx. every ⅝ (⅝-¾, ⅝-¾) in / 1.5 (1.5-2, 1.5-2) cm, K1, M1, knit until 2 sts rem, M1, k1. Increase the same way a total of 21 (20, 19) times = 84 (88, 92) sts. Continue until sleeve is given or desired length. Turn sleeve inside out and work 4 rows back and forth in stockinette for the facing. Loosely BO knitwise. Make the second sleeve the same way.

Finishing

Gently steam press the sweater. Measure and mark the depth of armhole to match the width across top of sleeve. Machine stitch armholes on each side of the center st at each side (see page 5). Carefully cut open armholes.

NOTE: The front and back are displaced by 1 stitch in relation to each other. Make sure to sew the seams so that the pattern matches on both sides of the armholes when finishing. Seam shoulders.

Collar
Worked with larger circular and 3 strands of Color 1 = 2 strands of Silk Mohair and 1 strand Alpaca Silk. The stitch count must be a multiple of 4. Work around in k2, p2 ribbing for 14¼ in / 36 cm. BO in ribbing.

Attach Sleeves
Pin each sleeve centered at the shoulder seam and underarm. Beginning at the shoulder, sew each side separately (sewing inside the facing).
Sew the facing down over the cut edges on the WS of each sleeve.

Weave in all ends neatly on WS.

Pattern A

Approx. 8¾ in / 22 cm

repeat   begin here

67

 Color 1: Charcoal Heather + Black
Color 2: White + Natural
Color 3: Acid Yellow + Acid Yellow

SOCKS

These socks are knitted with a very soft alpaca sock yarn and silk-mohair. Here are two versions using the same pattern. One has no patterning, but uses a contrast color for the heels and toes. The other pair features the *gásareygað*—"goose eye"—motif on the foot. Woolen socks and stockings played a major role in Faroese knitting history. At one time, stockings were the dominant currency in the Faroe Islands.

69

"A man is expected to spin from 1 to 1½ pounds, and, at the most, 2 pounds of wool a day.

"And a girl, ordinarily, can make or knit, while performing other household chores, 1 stocking; without such household chores, 1 pair. The most experienced girls can knit 3 stockings in a day; and there are even a few examples of girls who have outperformed that."

Svabo 1782

Sizes
Shoe sizes: U.S. 4-6 (7½-9, 10-12) / Euro 35-37 (38-40, 41-43)

Finished Measurements
Foot length: 8¾ (9½, 10¾) in / 22 (24, 27) cm
Sock leg length: 9½, (10¼, 11) in / 24 (26, 28) cm
All measurements refer to the finished garment sizing and are calculated with the listed gauge.

Materials
Yarn:
CYCA #1 (fingering) Sandnes Garn Alpaca Sock (70% alpaca, 30% nylon 218 yd/110 m / 50 g)
CYCA #4 (worsted, afghan, Aran) Sandnes Garn Silk Mohair (60% kid mohair, 25% silk, 15% wool, 306 yd/280 m / 50 g)

Color Suggestions:
Version 1:
Color 1: Alpaca Sock: Red 4219 + Silk Mohair: Strawberry 4065
Color 2: Alpaca Sock: Navy Blue 5575 + Silk Mohair: Strawberry 4065

Version 2:
Color 1: Alpaca Sock: Black 1099 + Silk Mohair: Black 1099
Color 2: Alpaca Sock: Natural 1012 + Silk Mohair: Natural 1012

Yarn Amounts:
Version 1:
Color 1: Alpaca Sock: 100 (100, 100) g +
Silk Mohair: 50 (50, 50) g
Color 2: Alpaca Sock: 50 (50, 50) g + Silk Mohair: included with Color 1
Version 2:
Color 1: Alpaca Sock: 100 (100, 100) g + Silk Mohair: 50 (50, 50) g
Color 2: Alpaca Sock: 50 (50, 50) g + Silk Mohair: 50 (50, 50) g

Needles
U.S. size 4 / 3.5 mm: set of 5 dpn

Gauge
20 sts in stockinette = 4 in / 10 cm
Adjust needle size to obtain correct gauge if necessary.

Version 1:
With dpn and Color 1 (= 1 strand of each yarn held together), CO 44 (48, 52) sts. Divide sts onto dpn and join; pm for beginning of rnd. Work around in k2, p2 ribbing until piece measures 9½ (10¼, 11) in / 24 (26, 28) cm. Place the center 19 (21, 23) sts on a holder for the instep. The rem 25 (27, 29) sts are used for the heel. Change to Color 2 (=1 strand of each yarn held together) and work back and forth in stockinette over the heel sts for 2 (2¼, 2½) in / 5 (5.5, 6) cm = heel flap. End with a WS row and pm on this row.

Heel Turn
Row 1 (RS): Knit across until 8 (9, 9) sts rem, sl 1, k1, psso; turn.
Row 2 (WS): Purl across until 8 (9, 9) sts rem, sl 1, p1, psso; turn.
Row 3 (RS): Knit across until 7 (8, 8) sts rem, sl 1, k1, psso; turn.
Row 4 (WS): Purl across until 7 (8, 8) sts rem, sl 1, p1, psso; turn.

Continue shaping the heel as est with 1 less st before deceasing on each pair of rows, until 11 (11, 11) sts rem.

Change to Color 1. Pick up and knit 8 (9, 10) sts on each side of the heel flap as you also place the 19 (21, 23) instep sts from holder onto dpn = 46 (50, 54) sts total. The beginning of the rnd is at the center of the heel/sole. Now work around in stockinette and, *at the same time*, shape the gusset: *Knit until 2 sts before instep, k2tog; work instep sts; ssk and knit to end of rnd. Knit 1 rnd*. Rep from * to * a total of 4 times = 38 (42, 46) sts rem. Continue around in stockinette until sock measures 6¾ (7½, 8¼) in / 17 (19, 21) cm from marker at the heel or to desired length before toe (allow approx. 2 (2, 2½) in / 5 (5, 6) cm for toe).

Change to Color 2. Pm at each side with 19 (21, 23) sts between markers. Working around in stockinette, decrease as follows: knit until 3 sts before 1st marker, k2tog, k1, sl m, k1, ssk; knit until 3 sts before 2nd marker, k2tog, k1, sl m, k1, ssk; knit to end of rnd. Knit 1 rnd. Decrease as est on every other rnd a total of 3 (3, 4) times and then decrease on every rnd 5 (6, 6) times = 6 sts rem for all sizes. Cut yarn and draw end through rem sts; tighten. Weave in all ends neatly on WS. Make the second sock the same way.

Version 2
Work as for Version 1 but work the heel flap and heel turn with Color 1. After turning the heel, pick up and knit sts along the heel flap with Color 1 = 1 rnd Color 1. Now continue as for Version 1, but work the 19 instep sts in Pattern A for all sizes. Work the rem 27 (31, 35) sts alternating k1 Color 2, k1 Color 1 = stripes. The first and last sts of Pattern A are a stripe in Color 1. Don't forget to shape the gusset as described for Version 1, but, decrease on each side of the center 19 instep sts for all sizes. Repeat this set-up of pattern until the foot measures 6¾ (7½, 8¼) in / 17 (19, 21) cm from the marker on the heel, or to desired length before toe (allow approx. 2 (2, 2½) in / 5 (5, 6) cm for toe). Change to Color 1, shape the toe and finish as for Version 1.

73

Color 1: Black + Black
Color 2: Natural + Natural

Pattern A

End here   begin here

repeat

"INNER SWEATER" MOTIFS

"Inner sweater" motifs are all striped. Narrow stripes alternate between blue with white motifs and white with blue motifs.

Historically, the term *undirtroyggja*—"inner sweater" or "under-sweater"—was used to refer to sweaters worn as inner garments by men, usually under a *vadmal* coat or vest.

SIGVALD

A man's sweater knitted in fine Norwegian wool yarn. This pattern has a round neck with an added rolled edge in a different color. The motif is called *úr Dalsgarði*— "from Dal's farm"—and was inspired by an old inner sweater worn by a Faroese fisherman. It's knitted in the traditional colors of white and blue, with a light, single-color lower edge. We've included a pattern for a matching single-color ribbed hat.

Sizes
S (M, L, XL, XXL)
Hat: One Size

Finished Measurements
Chest: 41¼ (43¼, 45¼, 47¼, 49¼) in / 105 (110, 115, 120, 125) cm
Length: 26¾ (27½, 28¼, 29¼, 30) in / 68 (70, 72, 74, 76) cm
Sleeve length: 20 (20½, 21, 21¼, 21¾) in / 51 (52, 53, 54, 55) cm or desired length.
Hat: circumference, approx. 20½ in / 52 cm when lightly stretched
All measurements refer to the finished garment sizing and are calculated with the listed gauge.

Materials
Yarn:
CYCA #2 (sport, baby) Sandnes Garn Tove (100% Norwegian wool, 175 yd/160 m / 50 g)

Colors:
Color 1: Natural Heather 2641
Color 2: Navy Blue 5575
Color 3: Dark Gray Heather 1053

Yarn Amounts:
Color 1: 300 (300, 350, 350, 400) g
Color 2: 300 (300, 350, 350, 400) g
Color 3: 50 (50, 50, 50, 50) g
Hat: Color 2: 100 g

Needles
U.S. sizes 2.5 and 4 / 3 and 3.5 mm: circulars and sets of 5 dpn

Gauge
24 sts in stockinette on larger needles = 4 in / 10 cm
Adjust needle sizes to obtain correct gauge if necessary.

78

Front and Back
With Color 1 and smaller circular, CO 252 (264, 276, 288, 300) sts. Join, being careful not to twist cast-on row; pm for beginning of rnd. Work around in stockinette for 2 in / 5 cm. Purl 1 rnd (foldline). All subsequent measurements for the body are taken from the foldline. Knit around in stockinette for another 2 in / 5 cm. Change to larger circular and Color 2. Purl 1 rnd. Change to Color 1 and knit 1 rnd. Change to Color 2 and purl 1 rnd = 2 ridges. Pm at each side with 127 (133, 139, 145, 151) sts for the front and 125 (131, 137, 143, 149) sts for the back. Continue around in stockinette and Pattern A. Begin at the arrow for your size. Work in pattern until piece measures approx. 23¾ (24½, 25¼, 25½, 26½) in / 60 (62, 64, 65, 67) cm from foldline. The sweater will look nicest if you end with a complete pattern panel.

Begin Neck Shaping: BO the center 21 (23, 25, 27, 29) sts for front neck. Complete the rnd and cut yarn. Now begin the rnd at center front. Work back and forth in stockinette and pattern. At neck edge, at the beginning of every row, BO 3,2,2,1,1,1,1,1 sts (for all sizes). *At the same time*, when the piece is approx. ⅝ in / 1.5 cm less than total length, at back: BO the center 41 (43, 45, 47, 49) sts for back neck. Work each side separately. At back neck edge, on every other row, BO 1,1 sts for all sizes = 40 (42, 44, 46, 48) sts rem for shoulder between the side sts and the neck on both front and back. Work until piece is given length and then BO all sts. We recommend ending at a complete pattern band for the most pleasing finish. Work the other side the same way, reversing shaping to match.

Sleeves
With Color 2 and smaller dpn, CO 52 (56, 56, 60, 60) sts. Join, being careful not to twist cast-on row; pm for beginning of rnd. Work around in k2, p2 ribbing for 2¾ in / 7 cm (all sizes). Change to larger dpn and Color 1. Knit 1 rnd, increasing 1 st = 53 (57, 57, 61, 61) sts. Change to Color 2 and purl 1 rnd. Change to Color 1 and knit 1 rnd; and then purl 1 rnd with Color 2 = 2 ridges. Now work around in stockinette and Pattern A. To determine the beginning of the rnd at underarm, count out from the arrow on the chart for the center of the sleeve. Make sure the pattern is centered on the sleeve.
Shape Sleeves: Work as follows: K1, M1, knit until 2 sts rem, M1, k1. Increase the same way approx. every ⅝ (⅝, ⅜-⅝, ⅝, ⅜- ⅝) in / 1.5 (1.5, 1-1.5, 1.5, 1-1.5) cm 29 (29, 31, 31, 33) times total = 111 (115, 119, 123, 127) sts. Continue until sleeve is given or desired length. It will look best if you end at a complete pattern panel. Knit 1 rnd in single-color stockinette with the background color for the last pattern panel.
Sleeve Facing: Turn sleeve inside out and, with the last-used color, work 5 rows back and forth in stockinette for the facing. Loosely BO knitwise. Make the second sleeve the same way.

Finishing
Gently steam press the sweater. Measure and mark the depth of armhole to match the width across top of sleeve. Machine stitch armhole on each side of the center st at each side (see page 5). Make sure that the patterns on body and sleeves match down the armholes. Carefully cut open armhole down the center stitch between the machine-stitching. Seam shoulders so that the pattern motifs match at the shoulder.

Fold facing at lower edge in at foldline and sew down on WS.

Neckband

With smaller circular and Color 2, pick up and knit 104 (108, 112, 116, 120) sts around the neck. The total stitch count must be a multiple of 4. Join and knit around in k2, p2 ribbing for about 2 in / 5 cm. Loosely BO in ribbing.

Rolled Collar around the Neckband

With smaller circular and Color 3, pick up and knit approx. 140 (145, 150, 155, 160) sts around the lower edge of the neck, where the ribbing meets the body of the sweater. Pm at the center of each shoulder. Knit 1 rnd. Now increase 1 st on each side of the marker at each side on every other rnd 2 times on each shoulder = 8 sts increased total. On the next rnd, BO loosely knitwise. The edge will roll inwards with the purl side showing outwards.

Attach Sleeves

Pin each sleeve around armhole, centered at the shoulder seam and at underarm. Beginning at shoulder seam, sew down each side separately, sewing inside the facing.

Sew the facing down over the cut edges on the WS of each sleeve.

Weave in all ends neatly on WS.

HAT

With Color 2 and smaller circular, CO 120 sts. Join, being careful not to twist cast-on row. Pm for beginning of rnd. Work around in k1, p1 ribbing until the hat measures approx. 13 in / 33 cm. On the next rnd, begin shaping the crown as follows:

NOTE: Change to dpn when sts no longer fit around circular.

Decrease Rnd 1: (10 sts in ribbing, k2tog) around = 10 sts decreased = 110 sts rem.

Work 1 rnd in ribbing (working knit over knit and purl over purl).

Decrease Rnd 2: (9 sts in ribbing, k2tog) around = 100 sts rem.

Work 1 rnd in ribbing (working knit over knit and purl over purl).

Rep the decrease rnds with 1 less st between decreases each time and the following ribbing rnd until 20 sts rem.

Last Decrease Rnd: (K2tog) around. Cut yarn, pull end through rem sts; tighten.

Weave in all ends neatly on WS.

79

Color 1: Natural Heather
Color 2: Navy Blue

Pattern A

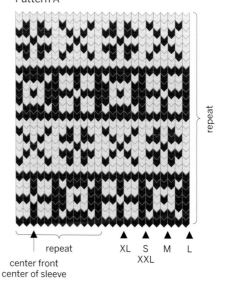

repeat

repeat
center front
center of sleeve

XL S M L
XXL

TRÓNDUR

A men's sweater knitted in thick soft
Norwegian wool. It features rolled edges
at the neck and sleeves. The motif on the
body is an inner-sweater pattern called
úr Múla—"from Múla," a tiny village in
the Faroe Islands. Two pattern panels run
across the chest; one is decorated with a
motif based on the *líttla stjørna*—"little
star"—pattern. This was inspired by a
Faroese national costume jacket owned
by Hans Marius Debes. The matching hat
complements the sweater perfectly.

Sizes
S (M, L, XL, XXL)
Hat: One Size

Finished Measurements
Chest: 38¼ (40½, 43¼, 46, 48½) in / 97 (103, 110, 117, 123) cm
Length: 26¾ (27½, 28¼, 29¼, 30) in / 68 (70, 72, 74, 76) cm
Sleeve length: 19¼ (19¾, 20, 20½, 21) in / 49 (50, 51, 52, 53) cm + rolled edge or desired length.
Hat: circumference, approx. 21 in / 53 cm
All measurements refer to the finished garment sizing and are calculated with the listed gauge.

Materials
Yarn:
CYCA #6 (Super Bulky) Sandnes Garn Easy (100% Norwegian wool, 55 yd/50 m / 50 g)

Colors:
Color 1: Navy Blue 6173
Color 2: Dark Gray Heather 1055
Color 3: Black 1099

Yarn Amounts:
Sweater:
Color 1: 500 (550, 600, 650, 700) g
Color 2: 300 (350, 400, 450, 500) g
Color 3: 50 (50, 50, 50, 50) g
Hat:
Color 1: 100 g
Color 2: 50 g or leftovers from sweater
Color 3: 50 g or leftovers from sweater

Needles
Sweater: U.S. sizes 10½ and 11 / 7 and 8 mm: circulars and sets of 5 dpn; U.S. size 10 / 6 mm: set of dpn for sleeve edges
Hat: U.S. sizes 10 and 11 / 6 and 8 mm: set of 5 dpn

Gauge
12 sts in stockinette on U.S. 11 / 8 mm needles = 4 in / 10 cm
Adjust needle sizes to obtain correct gauge if necessary.

Front and Back
With Color 1 and U.S. size 10½ / 7 mm circular, CO 108 (116, 124, 132, 140) sts. Join, being careful not to twist cast-on row; pm for beginning of rnd. Work around in k2, p2 ribbing for 2¾ in / 7 cm. Change to U.S. 11 / 8 mm circular and work around in stockinette and Pattern A. *On the first rnd,* increase 8 sts evenly spaced around = 116 (124, 132, 140, 148) sts.

Pm at each side with 58 (62, 66, 70, 74) sts each for front and back. Continue around in stockinette and Pattern A until piece measures approx. 15½ (16¼, 17, 17¾, 18½) in / 39 (41, 43, 45, 47) cm, ending the last "stripe" as shown on the chart. Now increase 1 st on each side of each side marker = 59 (63, 67, 71, 75) sts each for front and back.

Now work Pattern B, beginning and ending at the arrow for your size on each side. Next, work Pattern C the same way. When piece measures 25¼ (26, 26¾, 27½, 28¼) in / 64 (66, 68, 70, 72) cm, place the center 19 (19, 21, 21, 23) sts on a holder for the neck. Work back to the beginning of the rnd and cut yarn.

Begin again at the center front on the right side of the neck. Work back and forth in stockinette. At neck edge, place sts on holders as follows: at the beginning of each row at neck, 2,1,1 (2,1,1; 2,1,1; 2,2,1; 2,2,1). When about ¾ in / 2 cm from finished total length, also place the center back 25 (25, 27, 29, 31) sts on a holder for back neck. Work each side separately. Place 1 st on holder once = 16 (18, 19, 20, 21) sts rem for shoulder. Continue as est until piece is total length and then BO shoulder sts, leaving rem sts on holders.

Work the other side the same way, reversing shaping to match.

Sleeves
With Color 3 and U.S. size 10 / 6 mm dpn, CO 31 (33, 33, 33, 35) sts. Divide sts onto dpn and join, being careful not to twist cast-on row; pm for beginning of rnd. Work 4 rnds in stockinette + 1 purl rnd on RS = 1 ridge (foldline). All subsequent measurements are taken from this purl rnd. Change to U.S. 11 / 8 mm dpn and work around in stockinette and Pattern A. Note the center of the sleeve at the arrow on the chart and count back to determine the starting point for the rnd. *At the same time,* on the 1st rnd of pattern, decrease 4 sts evenly spaced around = 27 (29, 29, 29, 31) sts rem. Work in Pattern A for 1¼ in / 3 cm (all sizes) and then begin shaping sleeve. Every 1¼-1½ (1¼-1½, 1¼, 1¼, 1¼) in / 3-3.5 (3-3.5, 3, 3, 3) cm, increase as follows:
K1, M1, knit until 1 st rem, M1, k1.
Increase a total of 15 (15, 16, 17, 17) times = 57 (59, 61, 63, 65) sts.

Continue in Pattern A until sleeve measures 15¾ (16¼, 16½, 17, 17¼) in / 40 (41, 42, 43, 44) cm or approx. 3½ in / 9 cm before total desired length. End the last "stripe" as shown on the chart. Now work Pattern B. Note the arrow indicating the center of the sleeve and count back to the side to determine the beginning of the pattern. After completing Pattern B, knit 6 rnds with Color 1.
Sleeve Facing: Turn sleeve inside out and, with the last-used color, work 2 rows back and forth in stockinette for the facing. Loosely BO knitwise. Make the second sleeve the same way.

Finishing
Gently steam press the sweater. Measure and mark the depth of armhole to match the width across top of sleeve. Machine stitch armholes on each side of the center st at each side (see page 5). Carefully cut open armholes down the center stitch between the machine-stitching. Seam shoulders.

Neckband

Place held sts on U.S. 10½ / 7 mm circular and, with Color 1, pick up and knit extra sts from the neck shaping to the shoulder. Knit around in stockinette until neckband measures approx. 2½ in / 6 cm. Change to Color 3 and knit 1 rnd and then 1 purl rnd = 1 ridge. Knit 4 more rnds. Loosely BO knitwise. The neckband will roll at the top.

Attach Sleeves

Pin each sleeve around armhole centered at the shoulder seam and underarm. Beginning at the shoulder, sew each side separately, sewing inside the facing.

Sew the facing down over the cut edges on the WS of each sleeve.

Turn sleeve facings at foldline to WS and sew down smoothly.

Weave in all ends neatly on WS.

HAT

With Color 3 and U.S. size 10 / 6 mm circular, CO 64 sts. Join, being careful not to twist cast-on row. Pm for beginning of rnd. Knit 5 rnds and then purl 1 rnd = 1 ridge (foldline). Change to Color 2 and knit 1 rnd, purl 1 rnd = 1 ridge. All subsequent measurements are taken from the last purl rnd. Change to U.S. 11 / 8 mm circular and Color 1. Knit 9 rnds of Pattern A. After completing these rnds, continue with Color 1 until hat measures approx. 9½ in / 24 cm from purl line. On the next rnd, begin shaping the crown as follows:

Decrease Rnd 1: (K6, k2tog) around = 8 sts decreased = 56 sts rem.
Knit 1 rnd without decreasing.
Decrease Rnd 2: (K5, k2tog) around = 48 sts rem.
Knit 1 rnd without decreasing
On alternate rnds, rep the decrease rnd with 1 less st between decreases each time until 16 sts rem.
Last Decrease Rnd: (K2tog) around = 8 sts rem. Cut yarn, pull end through rem sts; tighten.
Fold facing at folding and sew down on WS. Weave in all ends neatly on WS.

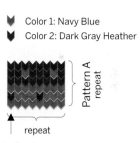

Color 1: Navy Blue
Color 2: Dark Gray Heather

Pattern A repeat

repeat

center front
center of sleeve

85

Pattern C

Pattern B

XXL XL L M S
end here

center front
center back
center of sleeve

S M L XL XXL
begin here

PANELS

A panel is a set-off pattern that repeats horizontally. Traditionally panels were used either individually or in combination with other motifs for sweaters, cardigans, and jackets.

ONE BIG FAMILY

A soft sweater for women and men, knitted in alpaca-wool and silk-mohair. The patterns are composed of panels and the fisherman's sweater motifs *stóra stjørna—* "large star"—and *krúnan—*"crown." It was once customary for every household to have its own distinct motif, and knitting somebody else's motif was frowned upon! Our inspiration was taken from that period: This sweater is teeming with different motifs, brought together to illustrate how we're all part of one big family. Matching hats are also included; one is in a single color, while the other features panels.

"The names 'Marjun pattern,' 'Todnes pattern,' and others remind me of a story I heard told in my youth. The son on a farm had married a young woman from another village. Back then, autumn was considered the most suitable season for celebrating a wedding. As soon as the festivities were over, everyone returned home and began preparing wool garments for Christmas. When the twentieth day of Christmas had passed, the young bride began to knit a sweater for her husband. When she had finished the first pattern, her mother-in-law came in and cried out when she saw the pattern, 'Lord, grant me strength. What are you thinking, Katrin, knitting a Stova motif for Jákup? This much I can tell you, these men [the members of the household] will not wear a sweater unless it's knitted with our pattern.' Katrin, who had neither the desire nor the courage to cross her mother-in-law, ripped out her work without a word and started again with the family's pattern. Each house in the village had its own pattern and no one used anyone else's pattern, even if it was ten times prettier, or so I've always heard. This custom died out a long time ago in the villages I know of, and I wouldn't think there is anyone nowadays, or at least there are very few people, who consider a pattern their property and won't let anyone else knit it ..."

Jóhanna Maria Skylv Hansen, 1933
Excerpt from a book review

Sizes
Sweater: XS (S, M, L, XL, XXL)
Women's Hat: One Size
Men's Hat: One Size

Finished Measurements
Sweater:
Chest: 35½ (38¼, 40½, 43¼, 46, 48½) in / 90 (97, 103, 110, 117, 123) cm
Length: 26 (26¾, 27½, 28¼, 29¼, 30) in / 66 (68, 70, 72, 74, 76) cm
Sleeve length: 18½ (19, 19¼, 19¾, 20, 20½) in / 47 (48, 49, 50, 51, 52) cm or desired length.
Hat: circumference approx. 21 in / 53 cm for women and approx. 22 in / 56 cm for men
All measurements refer to the finished garment sizing and are calculated with the listed gauge.

Materials
Yarn:
CYCA #4 (worsted, afghan, Aran) Sandnes Garn Alpakka Ull (65% alpaca, 35% wool, 109 yd/100 m / 50 g)
CYCA #4 (worsted, afghan, Aran) Sandnes Garn Silk Mohair (60% kid mohair, 25% silk, 15% wool, 306 yd/280 m / 50 g)

Color Suggestions:
Version 1:
Color 1: Alpakka Ull: Navy Blue 5575 + Silk Mohair: Deep Blue 6081
Color 2: Alpakka Ull: Beige Heather 2650 + Silk Mohair: Sand 2521
Color 3: Alpakka Ull: Petroleum 7572 + Silk Mohair: Petroleum 7572

Version 2
Color 1: Alpakka Ull: White 1002 + Silk Mohair: Natural 1012
Color 2: Alpakka Ull: Beige Heather 2650 + Silk Mohair: Sand 2521
Color 3: Alpakka Ull: Navy Blue 5575 + Silk Mohair: Deep Blue 6081

Yarn Amounts:
Sweater:
Color 1: Alpakka Ull: 300 (300, 350, 350, 400, 400) g + Silk Mohair: 100 (100, 150, 150, 150, 200) g
Color 2: Alpakka Ull: 200 (200, 250, 250, 300, 300) g + Silk Mohair: 50 (50, 100, 100, 100, 100) g
Color 3: Alpakka Ull: 100 (100, 150, 150, 200, 200) g + Silk Mohair: 50 (50, 50, 50, 50, 50) g

Men's Hat
Color 1: Alpakka Ull: 100g + Silk Mohair: 50 g or leftovers from sweater

Women's Hat
Color 1: Alpakka Ull: 100 g + Silk Mohair: 50 g or leftovers from sweater
Color 2: Alpakka Ull: 50 g or leftovers from sweater + Silk Mohair: 50 g or leftovers from sweater
Color 3: Alpakka Ull: 50 g or leftovers from sweater + Silk Mohair: 50 g or leftovers from sweater

Needles
U.S. sizes 6 and 8 or 9 / 4 and 5 or 5.5 mm: Circulars and sets of 5 dpn

Gauge
18 sts in stockinette on larger needles = 4 in / 10 cm
Adjust needle sizes to obtain correct gauge if necessary.

With Color 1 (= 1 strand of each yarn held together) and U.S. 6 / 4 mm circular, CO 164 (176, 188, 200, 212, 224) sts. Join, being careful not to twist cast-on row; pm for beginning of rnd. Work around in k2, p2 ribbing for 2¾ in / 7 cm. Change to large size circular (U.S 8 or 9 / 5 or 5.5 mm). Knit 1 rnd, decreasing 2 sts evenly spaced around = 162 (174, 186, 198, 210, 222) sts rem. Pm at each side with 81 (87, 93, 99, 105, 111) sts each for front and back. Beginning at the arrow for your size, work around in Pattern A. When piece measures 18¼ (18½, 19, 19¼, 19¾, 20) in / 46 (47 (48, 49, 50, 51) cm, begin armhole shaping. At each underarm, BO 3 sts on each side of each side marker = 6 sts bound off for each underarm. On the next rnd, CO 3 sts over each gap. These new sts form the armhole steeks (see page 5) which will be worked in a single-color; the 3 sts are not included in the stitch counts.

Continue around in pattern as est, and, *at the same time*, at armhole edges (before/after the 3 steek sts), on every other rnd, BO 2,2 (2,2; 2,2; 2,2,1; 2,2,1; 2,2,1) sts = 67 (73, 79, 83, 89, 95) sts rem.

Now continue without decreasing until piece measures 24½ (25¼, 26, 26¾, 27¼, 28) in / 62 (64, 66, 68, 69, 71) cm. BO the center front 21 (21, 23, 23, 25, 25) sts for front neck. Work back and forth and BO another 2,2,1 sts at neck edge on every row. *At the same time*, when piece measures ¾ in / 2 cm less than total length, BO the center back 29 (29, 31, 31, 33, 33) sts for back neck. Work each side separately and, on every other row, BO 1 more st at back neck = 18 (21, 23, 25, 27, 30) sts rem for shoulder. BO rem sts when body reaches finished length. Work the other side the same way, reversing shaping to match.

94

Sleeves

With Color 1 (= 1 strand of each yarn held together) and U.S. 6 / 4 mm dpn, CO 40 (40, 40, 44, 44, 44) sts. Join, being careful not to twist cast-on row; pm for beginning of rnd. Work around in k2, p2 ribbing for 2¾ in / 7 cm. Change to large size dpn (U.S 8 or 9 / 5 or 5.5 mm). Knit 1 rnd, increasing evenly spaced around to 41 (41, 43, 45, 45, 47) sts. Knit around in Pattern A. Set up pattern by calculating the center of the sleeve and aligning it with the arrow for center sleeve on the chart. Count back to determine beginning st of rnd.
Shape Sleeve: approx. every ¾-1 (¾-1, ¾-1, ¾-1, ¾, ¾, ¾) in / 2-2.5 (2-2.5, 2-2.5, 2-2.5, 2, 2) cm, increase 2 sts at underarm as follows: K1, M1, knit until 1 st rem, M1, k1. Increase the same way a total of 16 (17, 18, 19, 21, 22) times = 73 (75, 79, 83, 87, 91) sts. Work new sts into charted pattern as well as possible. When sleeve measures given or desired length, BO 6 sts centered at underarm. Now work back and forth and, at the beginning of each row, BO 2,2 (2,2; 2,2; 2,2,1; 2,2,1; 2,2,1) sts. BO rem sts. Make the second sleeve the same way.

Finishing

Gently steam press the sweater. Machine stitch armhole on each side of the center st of steek at each side). Carefully cut open armhole down the center stitch between the machine-stitching. Seam shoulders.

Neckband

With smaller circular and Color 1 (= 1 strand of each yarn), pick up and knit 80 (84, 88, 88, 92, 92) sts around neck. The stitch count must be a multiple of 4. Work around in k2, p2 ribbing for 7 in / 18 cm. BO in ribbing. Fold band to inside and sew down smoothly on WS.

Attach Sleeves

Pin each sleeve around armhole, centered at the shoulder seam and at underarm. Beginning at shoulder seam, sew down each side separately.

Facing at Sleeve Top

If you want a neat finish on the WS of the sleeves, you can knit a facing around the top of the sleeve that will cover the cut edges around the armhole. With larger dpn and 1 strand Alpakka Ull Color 1, pick up and knit about 9-10 sts for every 2 in / 5 cm from the base of underarm on body and around the entire armhole. Working back and forth, work 3 rows in stockinette and then BO loosely. **NOTE:** Make sure that the RS of the facing will face outwards once the facing folds over the raw edges when the sleeve is finished.

Weave in all ends neatly on WS.

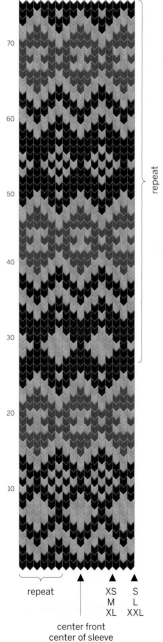

Pattern A

Color 1: Navy Blue + Deep Blue
Color 2: Beige Heather + Sand
Color 3: Petroleum + Petroleum

95

MEN'S HAT

With Color 1 (= 1 strand of each yarn) and U.S. size 6 / 4 mm circular, CO 92 sts. Join, being careful not to twist cast-on row. Pm for beginning of rnd. Work around in k2, p2 ribbing for 2 in / 5 cm. Change to U.S. 8 or 9 / 5 or 5.5 mm circular. Knit 1 rnd, increasing 7 sts evenly spaced around = 99 sts. Continue in stockinette around until hat measures approx. 9¾ in / 25 cm.

On the next rnd, begin shaping the crown as follows:
NOTE: Change to dpn when sts no longer fit around circular.
Decrease Rnd 1: (K9, k2tog) around = 9 sts decreased = 90 sts rem.
Knit 1 rnd without decreasing.
Decrease Rnd 2: (K8, k2tog) around = 81 sts rem.
Knit 1 rnd without decreasing.
Decrease Rnd 3: (K7, k2tog) around = 72 sts rem.
Knit 1 rnd without decreasing.
Last Decrease Rnd: (K2tog) around = 36 sts rem. Cut yarn, pull end through rem sts; tighten.
Weave in all ends neatly on WS.

WOMEN'S HAT

With Color 1 (= 1 strand of each yarn) and U.S. size 6 / 4 mm circular, CO 88 sts. Join, being careful not to twist cast-on row. Pm for beginning of rnd. Work around in k2, p2 ribbing for 2 in / 5 cm. Change to U.S. 8 or 9 / 5 or 5.5 mm circular. Knit 1 rnd, increasing 8 sts evenly spaced around = 96 sts. Continue around in Pattern B and then work the rest of the hat in Color 1. When hat measures approx. 9¾ in / 25 cm, on the next rnd, begin shaping the crown as follows:

NOTE: Change to dpn when sts no longer fit around circular.
Decrease Rnd 1: (K10, k2tog) around = 8 sts decreased = 88 sts rem.
Knit 1 rnd without decreasing.
Decrease Rnd 2: (K9, k2tog) around = 80 sts rem.
Knit 1 rnd without decreasing.
Decrease Rnd 3: (K8, k2tog) around = 72 sts rem.
Knit 1 rnd without decreasing.
Last Decrease Rnd: (K2tog) around = 36 sts rem. Cut yarn, pull end through rem sts; tighten.

Weave in all ends neatly on WS.

Pompom

With your choice of color, make a pompom, approx. 7 in / 18 cm in diameter. Sew pompom securely to top of hat.

Pattern B

repeat

 Color 1: White + Natural

Color 2: Beige Heather + Sand

Color 3: Navy Blue + Deep Blue

ONE BIG FAMILY—CHILDREN

A soft children's sweater, knitted with alpaca-wool and silk-mohair. The motifs are the same as for the adult sweaters, with the single addition of *kettunøsin*—the "cat's nose" motif. The matching hat features the same motifs.

Sizes
Sweater: 1-2 (3-4, 6, 8, 10, 12) years
Hat: 1-3 (4-6, 8-12) years

Finished Measurements
Sweater:
Chest: 22½ (24¾, 27½, 30¼, 32¾, 35½) in / 57 (63, 70, 77, 83, 90) cm
Length: 15 (16½, 18¼, 19¾, 21¼, 22¾) in / 38 (42, 46, 50, 54, 58) cm
Sleeve length: 10¼ (11½, 12¾, 13¾, 15, 16¼) in / 26 (29, 32, 35, 38, 41) cm or desired length.
Hat: circumference approx. 15¾ (18½, 21) in / 40 (47, 53) cm
All measurements refer to the finished garment sizing and are calculated with the listed gauge.

Materials
Yarn:
CYCA #4 (worsted, afghan, Aran)
Sandnes Garn Alpakka Ull (65% alpaca, 35% wool, 109 yd/100 m / 50 g)
CYCA #4 (worsted, afghan, Aran)
Sandnes Garn Silk Mohair (60% kid mohair, 25% silk, 15% wool, 306 yd/280 m / 50 g)

Color Suggestions
Version 1:
Color 1: Alpakka Ull: Navy Blue 5575 + Silk Mohair: Deep Blue 6081
Color 2: Alpakka Ull: White 1002 + Silk Mohair: Natural 1012
Color 3: Alpakka Ull: Beige Heather 2650 + Silk Mohair: Sand 2521

Version 2:
Color 1: Alpakka Ull: White 1002 + Silk Mohair: Natural 1012
Color 2: Alpakka Ull: Beige Heather 2650 + Silk Mohair: Sand 2521
Color 3: Alpakka Ull: Petroleum 7572 + Silk Mohair: Petroleum 7572

Yarn Amounts:
Sweater:
Color 1: Alpakka Ull: 100 (100, 150, 200, 200, 250) g + Silk Mohair: 50 (50, 50, 100, 100, 100) g
Color 2: Alpakka Ull: 50 (100, 100, 150, 150, 200) g + Silk Mohair: 50 (50, 50, 50, 50, 50) g
Color 3: Alpakka Ull: 50 (50, 50, 50, 100, 100) g + Silk Mohair: 50 (50, 50, 50, 50, 50) g

Hat
Color 1: Alpakka Ull: 50 g (all sizes) + Silk Mohair: 50 g or leftovers from sweater
Color 2: Alpakka Ull: 50 g (all sizes) + Silk Mohair: 50 g or leftovers from sweater
Color 3: Alpakka Ull: 50 g or leftovers from sweater + Silk Mohair: 50 g or leftovers from sweater

Needles
U.S. sizes 6 and 8 or 9 / 4 and 5 or 5.5 mm: Circulars and sets of 5 dpn

Gauge
18 sts in stockinette on larger needles = 4 in / 10 cm
Adjust needle sizes to obtain correct gauge if necessary.

NOTE: Read through the entire pattern before you start to knit because there are points at which several actions happen at the same time.

Front and Back
With Color 1 (= 1 strand of each yarn held together) and U.S. 6 / 4mm circular, CO 96 (108, 120, 132, 144, 156) sts. Join, being careful not to twist cast-on row; pm for beginning of rnd. Work around in k2, p2 ribbing for 1½ (1½, 2, 2 2½, 2½) in / 4 (4, 5, 5, 6, 6) cm. Change to large size circular (U.S 8 or 9 / 5 or 5.5 mm). Knit 1 rnd, increasing evenly spaced around to 102 (114, 126, 138, 150, 162) sts rem. Pm at each side with 51 (57, 63, 69, 75, 81) sts each for front and back. Beginning at the arrow for your size, work around in Pattern A. After completing Pattern A, begin Pattern B and, *at the same time*, adjust the stitch count on the first rnd to 105 (112, 126, 140, 147, 161), decreasing or increasing as necessary. It will look best if you increase or decrease at the sides. Note the arrow on the chart indicating the center front and count out to the beginning of the rnd to determine the starting point for Pattern B. On the last rnd in Pattern B, adjust the stitch count back to 102 (114, 126, 138, 150, 162) sts.

Now work the following sequence of patterns: *Pattern C, D, C, B*; rep from * to * until piece reaches total length. Don't forget to adjust the stitch count as described above every time you work Pattern B.

At the same time as working the pattern sequence, shape armholes when piece measures 9¾ (11, 12¼, 13, 14¼, 15½) in / 25 (28, 31, 33, 36, 39) cm. At each side, at the side markers, BO 2 sts on each side of each marker = 4 sts decreased at each side. On the next rnd, CO 3 new sts over the gap at each side. These new sts form the armhole steeks (see page 5) which will be worked in a single-color; the steek sts are not included in the stitch counts.

Pattern D

repeat

Pattern C

repeat

Hat Version 1

Pattern I

repeat

Hat Version 2

Pattern J

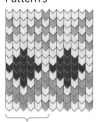

repeat

Pattern B

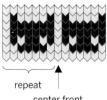

repeat

center front
center of sleeve

Pattern G

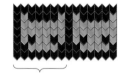

repeat

Pattern H

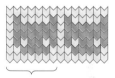

repeat

101

Pattern A

repeat

4   2
8   6
12   10

center front
center of sleeve

Pattern E

repeat

Pattern F

repeat

Version 1

Color 1: Navy Blue + Deep Blue
Color 2: White + Natural
Color 3: Beige Heather + Sand

Version 2

Color 1: White + Natural
Color 2: Beige Heather + Sand
Color 3: Petroleum + Petroleum

Continue around in pattern as est, and, *at the same time*, at armhole edges (before/after the 3 steek sts), on every other rnd, BO 1,1 (1,1; 1,1; 2,1; 2,1,1; 2,1,1) sts = 43 (49, 55, 59, 63, 69) sts rem each for front and back. The stitch count is calculated from Pattern C or D.
Now work without decreasing until piece measures 13 ½ (15, 16½, 18¼, 19¾, 21¼) in / 34 (38, 42, 46, 50, 54) cm. BO the center front 13 (13, 15, 15, 17, 17) sts for front neck. Work back and forth and, at beginning of every row, BO 2,1 sts (all sizes). *At the same time,* when piece is ¾ in / 2 cm less than total length, BO the center back 17 (17, 19, 19, 21, 21) sts for back neck. Work each side separately and, on every other row at back neck, decrease 1 st = 12 (15, 17, 19, 20, 23) sts rem for each shoulder. The stitch counts are taken in Pattern C or D. BO when piece measures given total length. Work the other side the same way, reversing shaping to match.

Sleeves

With Color 1 (= 1 strand of each yarn held together) and U.S. 6 / 4 mm dpn, CO 28 (32, 32, 36, 36, 36) sts. Join, being careful not to twist cast-on row; pm for beginning of rnd. Work around in k2, p2 ribbing for 2 in / 5 cm. Change to larger dpn (U.S 8 or 9 / 5 or 5.5 mm). Knit 1 rnd, increasing evenly spaced around to 29 (33, 35, 37, 37, 39) sts. Knit around in the same sequence of charted patterns as for the body. Set up patterns by calculating the center of the sleeve and aligning it with the arrow for center of sleeve on the chart. Count back to determine beginning st of rnd.
Shape Sleeve: approx. every ¾-1 (1, 1, 1, ¾-1, ¾-1) in / 2-2.5 (2.5, 2.5, 2.5, 2-2.5, 2-2.5) cm, increase 2 sts at underarm as follows: K1, M1, knit until 1 st rem, M1, k1. Increase the same way a total of 9 (9, 10, 12, 14, 15) times = 47 (51, 55, 61, 65, 69) sts. Work new sts into charted pattern as well as possible.

When sleeve measures given or desired length, BO 4 sts centered at underarm. Now work back and forth and, at the beginning of each row, BO 1,1 (1,1; 1,1; 2, 1; 2,1,1; 2,1,1) sts. BO rem sts. Make the second sleeve the same way.

Finishing

Gently steam press the sweater. Machine stitch armholes on each side of the center steek st at each side. Carefully cut open armholes down the center stitch between the machine-stitching. Seam shoulders.

Neckband

With smaller circular and Color 1 (= 1 strand of each yarn), pick up and knit 60 (64, 68, 68, 72, 76) sts around neck. The stitch count must be a multiple of 4. Work around in k2, p2 ribbing for 3¼ (4, 4, 4¾, 4¾, 4¾) in / 8 (10, 10, 12, 12, 12) cm. BO in ribbing. Fold band to inside and sew down smoothly on WS.

Attach Sleeves

Pin each sleeve around armhole, centered at the shoulder seam and at underarm. Beginning at shoulder seam, sew down each side separately.

Facing at Sleeve Top

If you want a neat finish on the WS of the sleeves, you can knit a facing around the top of the sleeve that will cover the cut edges around the armhole. With larger dpn and 1 strand Alpakka Ull Color 1, pick up and knit about 9-10 sts for every 2 in / 5 cm from the base of underarm on body and around the entire armhole. Working back and forth, work 3 rows in stockinette and then BO loosely.
NOTE: Make sure that the RS of the facing will face outwards once the facing is folded over the raw edges when the sleeve is finished.

Weave in all ends neatly on WS.

HAT

With Color 1 (= 1 strand of each yarn) and U.S. size 6 / 4 mm circular, CO 72 (84, 96) sts. Join, being careful not to twist cast-on row. Pm for beginning of rnd. Work around in k2, p2 ribbing for 1¼ (1¼, 1½) in / 3 (3, 4) cm. Change to U.S. 8 or 9 / 5 or 5.5 mm circular. Knit 1 rnd. Work around in Pattern E for Version 1 or Pattern F for Version 2. Next, work Pattern G for Version 1 or Pattern H for Version 2, adjusting the stitch count on the first rnd to 70 (84, 98) sts by increasing/decreasing as necessary. On the last rnd of Pattern G or H, adjust the stitch count back to 72 (84, 96) sts.
Size 1-3 years: work the rest of the hat with Color 1.
Sizes 4-6 (8-12) years: work Pattern I for Version 1 or Pattern J for Version 2 and then work the rest of the hat with Color 1.

When hat measures 5½ (7, 8) in / 14 (18, 20) cm, begin shaping crown as follows:
NOTE: Change to dpn when sts no longer fit around circular.
Decrease Rnd 1: (K10, k2tog) around = 6 (7, 8) sts decreased = 66 (77, 88) sts rem.
Knit 1 rnd without decreasing.
Decrease Rnd 2: (K9, k2tog) around = 6 (7, 8) sts decreased = 60 (70, 80) sts rem. Knit 1 rnd without decreasing.
Decrease Rnd 3: (K8, k2tog) around = 54 (63, 72) sts rem.
Knit 1 rnd without decreasing.
Last Decrease Rnd: (K2tog) around = 27 (32, 36) sts rem. Cut yarn, pull end through rem sts; tighten.
Weave in all ends neatly on WS.

Pompom

With your choice of color, make a pompom, approx. 3½ in / 9 cm in diameter. Sew pompom securely to top of hat.

SANDOYARGENTAN

A women's sweater with raglan shaping, knitted in soft heavy Norwegian wool yarn. The design is made up of panels with a selection of small motifs. Tailor Debes told a story about a girl from the island of Sandoy who sent her grandmother some orchil dye as a gift. It must have been made from quality lichen, because the first dyebath yielded a vibrant violet, the second a cherry red, and the third time the usual orchil color. There's also a matching hat with a rolled edge, motifs, and a large pompom.

"... after they befriended each other on St. Olaf's Day (July 29th), my grandmother and the girl from Sandoy never met again on this earth; but they did send each other little gifts. Just before one of the first Christmases after they had met, a large pod of pilot whales was herded into Funningsfjørður, and people came from Sandoy for a share of the whale meat and blubber. Grandmother's friend sent her a gift with one of the whalers—orchil that she herself had prepared. The day before Christmas Eve, Grandmother used it to dye, and it was so potent that the first time she dyed, it yielded a vibrant violet; the second time, cherry red; and the third time, the usual orchil color."

Excerpt from the story "My Grandmother Was in Tórshavn One St. Olaf's Day" in *Tales of the Old Days* by Hans M. Debes.

Sizes
Sweater: S (M, L, XL)
Hat: One Size

Finished Measurements
Sweater:
Chest: 33½ (37½, 41¼, 45¼) in / 85 (95, 105, 115) cm
Length: 24¾ (25½, 26½, 27¼) in / 63 (65, 67, 69) cm
Sleeve length: 18¼ (18½, 19, 19¼) in / 46 (47, 48, 49) cm + rolled edge or desired length.
Hat: circumference, approx. 19¾ in / 50 cm when lightly stretched
All measurements refer to the finished garment sizing and are calculated with the listed gauge.

Materials
Yarn:
CYCA #6 (Super Bulky) Sandnes Garn Easy (100% Norwegian wool, 55 yd/50 m / 50 g)

Colors:
Color 1: Light Gray Heather 1032
Color 2: Burgundy 4554
Color 3: Deark Heather 4855

Yarn Amounts:
Color 1: 450 (500, 550, 600) g
Color 2: 50 (100, 100, 100) g
Color 3: 50 (50, 50, 100) g

Hat
Color 1: 100 g + 50 g for pompom
Color 2: 50 g or leftovers
Color 3: 50 g or leftovers

Needles
Sweater
U.S. sizes 10½ and 11 / 7 and 8 mm: circulars and sets of 5 dpn;
U.S. size 10 / 6 mm for sleeve cuffs: set of 5 dpn
Hat: U.S. sizes 10 and 11 / 6 and 8 mm: set of 5 dpn

Gauge
12 sts and 14 rnds in pattern or 16 rnds in stockinette on larger needles = 4 in / 10 cm
Adjust needle sizes to obtain correct gauge if necessary.

Front and Back
With Color 1 and U.S. size 10½ / 7 mm circular, CO 104 (116, 128, 140) sts. Join, being careful not to twist cast-on row; pm for beginning of rnd. Work around in k2, p2 ribbing for 2¾ in / 7 cm. Change to U.S. 11 / 8 mm circular and work around in stockinette and, on the first rnd, decrease 2 sts evenly spaced around = 102 (114, 126, 138) sts. Pm at each side with 51 (57, 63, 69) sts each for front and back. Continue around in stockinette until piece measures approx. 11½ (11¾, 12¼, 12¾) in / 29 (30, 31, 32) cm. Now begin Pattern A at the arrow for your size. After completing Pattern A, work Pattern B, beginning and ending at the arrow for your size at each side as shown on the chart.

When piece measures 17¼ (17¾, 18¼, 18½) in / 44 (45, 46, 47) cm, bind off for underarm: BO 4 sts at each side of each side marker = 8 sts bound off at each side of body. Set body aside while you knit the sleeves.

Sleeves
With Color 3 and U.S. 10 / 6 mm dpn, CO 27 (29, 29, 31) sts. Join, being careful not to twist cast-on row; pm for beginning of rnd. Knit 5 rnds in stockinette + 1 purl rnd = 1 ridge for the foldline. All subsequent measurements are taken from the foldline. Change to Color 2, knit 1 rnd, purl 1 rnd = 1 ridge. Change to dpn U.S. 11 / 8 mm and Color 1. Work around in stockinette and Pattern C and, *on the first rnd*, decrease 4 sts evenly spaced around = 23 (25 25, 27) sts. Note the arrow indicating the center of the sleeve on the chart and count out sts from center of sleeve to determine the beginning of the pattern.
Shape Sleeve: approx. every 2¼ (2¼, 2, 2) in / 5.5 (5.5, 5, 5) cm, increase 2 sts at underarm as follows: K1, M1, knit until 1 st rem, M1, k1. Increase the same way a total of 8 (8, 9, 9) times = 39 (41, 43, 45) sts. After completing Pattern

C, continue with Color 1 until sleeve measures approx. 12¾ (13, 13½, 13¾) in/ 32 (33, 34, 35) cm or about 5½ in / 14 cm before desired total length. Work Pattern A and then Pattern B. Use the arrow indicating center of sleeve on the chart to calculate where to begin pattern rnd on the sleeve. Work until sleeve measures given or desired total length and end on the same pattern rnd as for front and back. BO 4 sts on each side of underarm marker = 8 sts bound off. Set sleeve aside while you make another sleeve the same way.

Raglan Shaping
Arrange the pieces on U.S. 11 / 8 mm circular in this order: back, one sleeve, front, second sleeve = a total of 148 (164, 180, 196) sts. Pm at each intersection of body and sleeve = 4 markers. Rnd begins at the back. Work in Pattern B over all the sts as before (note that the pattern will not match at raglan shaping lines).
Shape Raglan: Beginning at back, k2tog, work until 2 sts before next marker, ssk, sl m, k2tog, *work until 2 sts before next marker, k2tog, sl m, ssk; rep from * at each marker around = 8 sts decreased around. Work decreases with the color that fits best into pattern. Knit 2 rnds without decreasing.

Continue by decreasing on every 3rd rnd 4 times total. After completing Pattern B, continue with Color 1 only. Now decrease on evey other rnd 7 (8, 9, 10) times = a total of 11 (12, 13, 14) raglan decrease rnds and 21 (25, 29, 33) sts rem between markers for front and back and 9 sts rem for each sleeve.

Place the center 11 (13,15, 17) sts at front on a holder. Work to beginning of rnd and cut yarn. Now begin at center front on the right side of the neck. Work back and forth in stockinette, shaping raglan as before. *At the same time*, place 1 st at beginning of every row onto a holder until all the sts of the front have been decreased away or held. Leave rem sts on the circular.

Neckband

Slip sts to U.S. 10½ / 7 mm circular + the held sts. Join and work around in stockinette until neckband measures approx. 1½ in / 4 cm. Change to U.S. 10 / 6 mm circular and Color 2. Knit 1 rnd, purl 1 rnd = 1 ridge. Change to Color 3; knit 1 rnd, purl 1 rnd = 1 ridge. Continue with Color 3 and knit 5 rnds. Loosely BO knitwise. The top of the neckband will roll forward a little.

Finishing

Gently steam press sweater. Seam underarms. Weave in all ends neatly on WS.

HAT

With Color 3 and U.S. size 10 / 6

mm circular, CO 60 sts. Join, being careful not to twist cast-on row. Pm for beginning of rnd. Knit 5 rnds in stockinette + 1 purl rnd = 1 ridge. Change to Color 2 and knit 1 rnd, purl 1 rnd = 1 ridge. All subsequent measurements are taken from this ridge. Change to U.S. 11 / 8 mm circular and Color 1. Work around in Pattern C. After completing Pattern C, continue with Color 1 only. When hat measures 6 in / 15 cm from ridge, begin shaping top as follows:
NOTE: Change to dpn when sts no longer fit around circular.
Decrease Rnd 1: (K8, ssk) around = 6 sts decreased = 54 sts rem.
Knit 1 rnd without decreasing.
Decrease Rnd 2: (K7, ssk) around = 6 sts decreased = 48 sts rem.
Knit 1 rnd without decreasing.
Decrease Rnd 3: (K6, ssk) around = 42 sts rem.
Knit 1 rnd without decreasing.

Decrease Rnd 4: (K5, ssk) around = 36 sts rem.
Knit 1 rnd without decreasing.
Decrease Rnd 5: (K4, ssk) around = 30 sts rem.
Decrease Rnd 6: (K3, ssk) around = 24 sts rem.
Last Decrease Rnd: (Ssk) around = 12 sts rem. Cut yarn, pull end through rem sts; tighten.

Weave in all ends neatly on WS.

Pompom

With Color 1, make a large pompom, approx. 8 in / 20 cm in diameter. Sew pompom securely to top of hat. With your hands protected, hold the pompom over boiling water and steam it until it fluffs out.

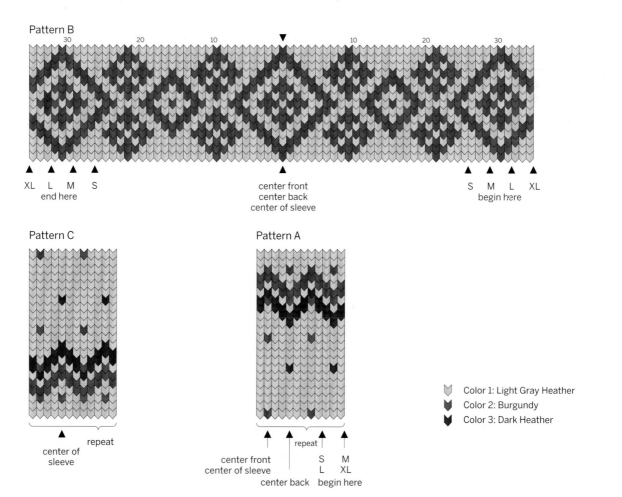

MALENA

A flowing women's cardigan with raglan shaping, knitted in alpaca-wool and silk-mohair. The front bands and pocket edgings are worked in seed stitch. The design is a combination of six different panels and was inspired by one of Tailor Debes's tales of a young woman who visited the wealthy á Látrið farm for Christmas. Her hosts let her have the duvet the Danish Crown Prince had used when he visited the Faroe Islands in 1844. Back home she wanted it to be known that she had been in royal company, and so would bid everyone goodnight in Danish.

Sizes
Sweater: XS-S (M, L-XL)

Finished Measurements
Chest: 40¼ (44, 48) in / 102 (112, 122) cm
Length: 28¼ (29½, 30¾) in / 72 (75, 78) cm
Sleeve length: approx. 17¾ (18¼, 18½) in / 45 (46, 47) cm
All measurements refer to the finished garment sizing and are calculated with the listed gauge.

Materials
Yarn:
CYCA #2 (sport, baby) Sandnes Garn Tynn Alpakka Ull (65% alpaca, 35% wool, 182 yd/166 m / 50 g)
CYCA #4 (worsted, afghan, Aran) Sandnes Garn Silk Mohair (60% kid mohair, 25% silk, 15% wool, 306 yd/280 m / 50 g)

Color Suggestions:
Color 1: Tynn Alpakka Ull: Charcoal Heather 1088 + Silk Mohair: Ink Blue 6863
Color 2: Tynn Alpakka Ull: Strawberry Red 4237 + Silk Mohair: Burgundy 4545
Color 3: Tynn Alpakka Ull: White 1002 + Silk Mohair: Natural 1012

Yarn Amounts:
Color 1: Tynn Alpakka Ull: 350 (400, 450) g + Silk Mohair: 200 (200, 250) g
Color 2: Tynn Alpakka Ull: 200 (200, 250) g + Silk Mohair: 50 (50, 100) g
Color 3: Tynn Alpakka Ull: 50 (50, 50) g + Silk Mohair: 50 (50, 50) g

Needles
U.S. sizes 6 and 8 / 4 and 5 mm: Circulars and sets of 5 dpn

Gauge
20 sts and 20 rnds in two-color stranded pattern on larger needles = 4 in / 10 cm
Adjust needle sizes to obtain correct gauge if necessary.

NOTES: If you knit single color stockinette more loosely than two-color pattern knitting, use needles one U.S. or one-half metric size smaller when working in stockinette.
Read through the entire pattern before you start to knit because there are points at which several actions happen at the same time.

SEED STITCH
Row/Rnd 1: (K1, p1) around or across.
Row/Rnd 2 and all subsequent rows/rnds: Work purl over knit and knit over purl.

Front and Back
With Color 1 (= 1 strand of each yarn held together) and smaller circular, CO 218 (238, 258) sts. Pm at beginning of row for one side and at opposite side with 102 (112, 122) sts for the back and 116 (126, 136) sts for the front. Work back and forth as follows:

Row 1 (WS): Work in seed st over the first 14 sts and then work (k2, p2) ribbing until 14 sts rem; end with 14 sts in seed st.

Row 2 (RS): Work 14 sts in seed st, (p2, k2) ribbing until 14 sts rem, and end with 14 sts in seed st.

Row 3: Work 14 sts in seed st, p10, 34 seed sts, purl until 58 sts rem, 34 seed sts, p10, 14 seed sts.

Row 4: Work 14 sts in seed st, k10, 34 seed sts, knit until 58 sts rem, 34 seed sts, k10, 14 seed sts.

Rep Rows 3-4 until piece measures 6¼ (6¾, 7) in / 16 (17, 18) cm. On next WS row, BO for pocket opening: 14 seed sts, p10, BO the next 34 sts in seed st, purl until 58 sts rem, BO 34 sts in seed st, p10, 14 seed sts. Set piece aside and make pocket linings.

Pocket Lining
With Color 1 (= 1 strand of each yarn held together) and smaller circular, CO 34 sts. Work back and forth in seed st until pocket is same measurement as body above ribbing. Set piece aside. Make another pocket lining the same way. Now join the linings to the body on the next RS row: Place the first 14 sts in seed st on a holder = front band which will be worked later when finishing. K10, k34 with the first lining, knit until 58 sts rem. Knit 34 sts of lining, k10, and place the last 14 sts on a holder for front band to be worked in finishing.

Now join to work the jacket in the round: Change to larger circular. CO 3 new sts at end of row for the steek (see page 5). The steek sts will later be cut open for the front opening. Always work steek sts in a single color. Steek sts are not included in stitch counts.
Work 1 rnd in stockinette with Color 1 and, *at the same time*, decrease 1 st at about the center back = 189 (209, 229) sts rem. Now work Pattern A. Begin the rnd at the arrow for your size.
Knit 2 rnds with Color 1.
Work Pattern B.
Knit 2 rnds with Color 1.
Work Pattern C.
Knit 1 rnd with Color 1.
Work Pattern D.
Knit 1 rnd with Color 1.
Work Pattern E.
Knit 2 rnds with Color 1.
Work Pattern B.
Knit 2 rnds with Color 1.
Work Pattern F.
Knit 2 rnds with Color 1.
Work Pattern G.
Knit 2 rnds with Color 1.

NOTE: The V-neck opening begins here, approximately. See *At the Same Time* below.

Work Pattern A.
Knit 2 rnds with Color 1.
Work Pattern B.
Knit 2 rnds with Color 1.
Work Pattern H.
Knit 2 rnds with Color 1.
Work Pattern F.

At the same time, when piece measures 19 (19¾, 20½) in / 48 (50, 52) cm, begin shaping neck. Decrease after/before the 3 steek sts at center front: K1, k2tog, knit until 3 sts rem (before steek), ssk, k1. Decrease the same way about every ¾ in / 2 cm (all sizes). *At the same time*, when piece measures 20½ (21, 21¼) in / 52 (53, 54) cm, shape armholes at each side: BO 4 sts on each side of each side marker = 16 sts decreased on rnd (8 sts decreased at each armhole) = 93 (103, 113) sts rem for back with rem sts for front. Set body aside while you make the sleeves.

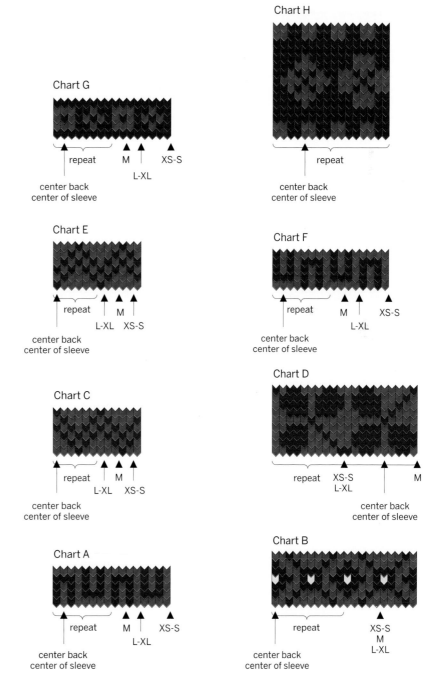

115

Color 1: Charcoal Heather + Ink Blue
Color 2: Strawberry Red + Burgundy
Color 3: White + Natural

Sleeves

With Color 1 (= 1 strand of each yarn held together) and smaller dpn, CO 36 (40, 40) sts. Divide sts onto dpn and join to work in the rnd; pm for beginning of rnd. Work 2 rnds in k2, p2 ribbing. Change to larger dpn and continue around in stockinette, increasing on the first rnd 11 (11, 15) sts evenly spaced around = 47 (51, 55) sts. Every approx. 1¼ in / 3 cm (all sizes), increase as follows: K1, M1, knit until 1 st rem, M1, k1. Increase a total of 13 (13, 13) times for all sizes = 73 (77, 81) sts. *At the same time*, when sleeve measures 5¼ (5½, 6) in / 13 (14, 15) cm, work in same charted pattern sequence as for body, but *begin with Pattern B* so that the patterns will match those on the body for the entire sleeve length. To calculate beginning of pattern, see arrow on chart for center of sleeve and count back. Continue as est until sleeve is given or desired length to underarm, ending on the same rnd for for front/back. BO 8 sts centered on underarm = 65 (69, 73) sts rem. Set sleeve aside and make the second sleeve the same way.

Raglan Shaping

Place the stitches around the larger circular: front, one sleeve, back, second sleeve. Pm at each intersection of body and sleeve = 4 markers. Begin rnd at center front as before. Work the yoke in the round in the pattern sequence as est. However, when you are about to begin Pattern H, count out from the center back and on the sleeves to determine where to begin the pattern. Also, work the left front mirror image to the right front. Decrease for the raglan shaping on every other rnd and, *at the same time*, continue shaping V-neck as follows:
Before each marker: ssk.
After each marker: k2tog.
On every decrease rnd, there will be 8 decreases + the V-neck decreases. Decrease with the color that works best with the pattern. Note that the pattern will not stay in sequence at the intersections of body and sleeves. After completing Pattern F, continue with only Color 1 and stockinette.

Decrease a total of 11 (12, 13) times on each side for the V-neck and a total of 28 (30, 32) raglan decrease rnds = 57 (67, 77) sts rem. BO rem sts.

Finishing

Gently steam press garment. Machine stitch center front steek on each side of the center stitch (see page 5). Carefully cut open down the center stitch between the machine-stitching.

Left Front Band

Slip the sts from the holder onto smaller needles. Continue in seed st over the outermost 14 sts and then CO 2 new sts on the side next to front edge of body. These two sts are facing stitches which will be sewn over the cut edge later. Work these two sts in reverse stockinette: purl on RS and knit on WS. This allows the stockinette side to be visible on the wrong side when the edge is sewn over the cut edges. Make sure to tighten the yarn slightly at the beginning of every row so the edges will be firm and neat.

When the band reaches the top end of the steek, BO the facing sts. Continue in seed st until the front band reaches the center back neck without stretching. It is better to make the band a little too long than too short so you don't have to add a few rows when joining the band to the jacket. BO.

Right Front Band

Work mirror-image to left front band.

Sew the front bands smoothly along the front edge of the jacket. Seam the short ends of the bands at back neck. Sew the facings over the cut edges. Seam underarms. Sew the pocket linings to the inside of the fronts, at each side and along the cast-on edge. Weave in all ends neatly on WS.

ELIN

A women's short fitted sweater knitted
in fine alpaca-wool yarn. This design has
plackets with buttons at the neck and
on the cuffs. The pattern is composed of
women's sweater motifs in both horizontal
and vertical panels. The idea for this
design came from Tailor Debes's tale of
a woman ahead of her time. She didn't
walk to church services, but rather arrived
on horseback. She also wove and crafted
suspenders and stocking bands for export
to "foreign lands."

Sizes
Sweater: XS-S (M, L-XL)

Finished Measurements
Chest: 34¾ (39¾, 45) in / 88 (101, 114) cm
Length: 22¾ (23¾, 24½) in / 58 (60, 62) cm
Sleeve length: 17¼ (17¾, 18¼) in / 44 (45, 46) cm or desired length
All measurements refer to the finished garment sizing and are calculated with the listed gauge.

MATERIALS
Yarn:
CYCA #2 (sport, baby) Sandnes Garn Tynn Alpakka Ull (65% alpaca, 35% wool, 182 yd/166 m / 50 g)

Color Suggestions:
Color 1: Tynn Alpakka Ull: Black 1099
Color 2: Tynn Alpakka Ull: Strawberry Red 4237

Yarn Amounts:
Color 1: Tynn Alpakka Ull: 250 (250, 300) g
Color 2: Tynn Alpakka Ull: 200 (250, 250) g

Notions
5 buttons

Needles
U.S. sizes 1.5 and 2.5 or 4 / 2.5 and 3 or 3.5 mm: Circulars and sets of 5 dpn

Gauge
25 sts and 28 rows in two-color stranded pattern on larger needles = 4 in / 10 cm
Adjust needle sizes to obtain correct gauge if necessary.

Front and Back
With Color 1 and smaller circular, CO 220 (252, 280) sts. Join, being careful not to twist cast-on row. Pm for beginning of rnd. Work garter st in the round: purl 1 rnd, knit 1 rnd, purl 1 rnd = 2 ridges. Now work 8 rnds in stockinette. Change to larger needles. Work Pattern A. On the last rnd of Pattern A, decrease 1 st at each side for size M only. Next, work Pattern B. On the last rnd of Pattern B, increase 1 st at each side for size M only. Work Pattern A, increasing 2 sts at each side for size L-XL on the last rnd = 220 (252, 284) sts. Pm at each side with 110 (126, 142) sts each for front and back. Continue working around as follows:
NOTE: The pattern will not match at both sides of the side markers but will be adjusted when the pieces are separated for back and front.

Over the sts of the front, after the first side marker: work Pattern C, Pattern D over the next 16 (24, 32) sts, Pattern E, Pattern F over the last 16 (14, 32) sts.

On the back, after the second side marker: work Pattern C and then Pattern D over the next 105 (121, 137) sts. Rep these panels as est until piece measures 15 (15½, 15¾) in / 38 (39, 40) cm. BO the center st of Pattern C + 5 sts on each side of the center st for the underarm = 11 sts bound off at each side. On the next rnd, CO 4 new sts over the gap at each side for the armhole steeks (see page 5). Always work the steek sts in a single color. Steek sts are not included in any stitch counts.
Shape Armholes: On every other rnd, decrease on each side of the steek sts. On the first decrease rnd, on each side of steek, sl 1, k2tog, psso = 2 sts decreased. On the next 3 decrease rnds: K2tog on each side of steek = total of 5 sts decreased on each side = 89 (105, 121) sts rem each on front and back.

Continue without decreasing until piece measures 17¼ (18¼, 19) in / 44 (46, 48) cm. BO the center 3 front sts for the front placket. Now either work back and forth or CO 4 new sts over the gap for a steek so you can continue in the round. Always work the steek sts in a single color. Steek sts are not included in any stitch counts. Work until piece measures 20 (21, 21¾) in / 51 (53, 55) cm and then shape neck: BO the 4 steek sts at center front if you were working in the round. Work back and forth and, on every row at neck edge, BO 16,2,1,1,1,1,1 (16,2,1,1,1,1,1,1; 17,2,2,1,1,1,1,1,1) sts. *At the same time*, when piece is ¾ in / 2 cm less than total length, BO the center 49 (51, 57) sts for back neck = 20 (27, 32) sts rem for each back shoulder. Work each side separately and shape shoulder by binding off 7,7,6 (9,9,9; 11,11,10) sts from outer edge. BO steek sts. Work the other side the same way, reversing shaping to match.

Sleeves
With smaller circular and Color 1, CO 54 (54, 54) sts. Knit 3 rows back and forth = 2 ridges. Still working back and forth, work 8 rows in stockinette. The first and last st is an edge st and is always knitted on all rows. Change to larger circular and work Pattern A back and forth. On the last row of Pattern A, decrease 2 sts at the center of the sleeve with 2 sts between the decreases (= the center of underarm when the sleeve is later worked in the round). Work Pattern B back and forth and, on the last row, increase 2 sts with 2 sts in between the increases. Still working back and forth, work Pattern A. Now join to work in the round (use dpn or short circular). The rnd begins at the center of the piece. Knit 1 rnd with Color 1 and, *at the same time*, increase 1 (3, 5) sts evenly spaced around = 55 (57, 59) sts. Work Pattern B. Note the arrow on the chart for the center of the sleeve (= center of the placket) and count out from

Color 1: Black
Color 2: Strawberry Red

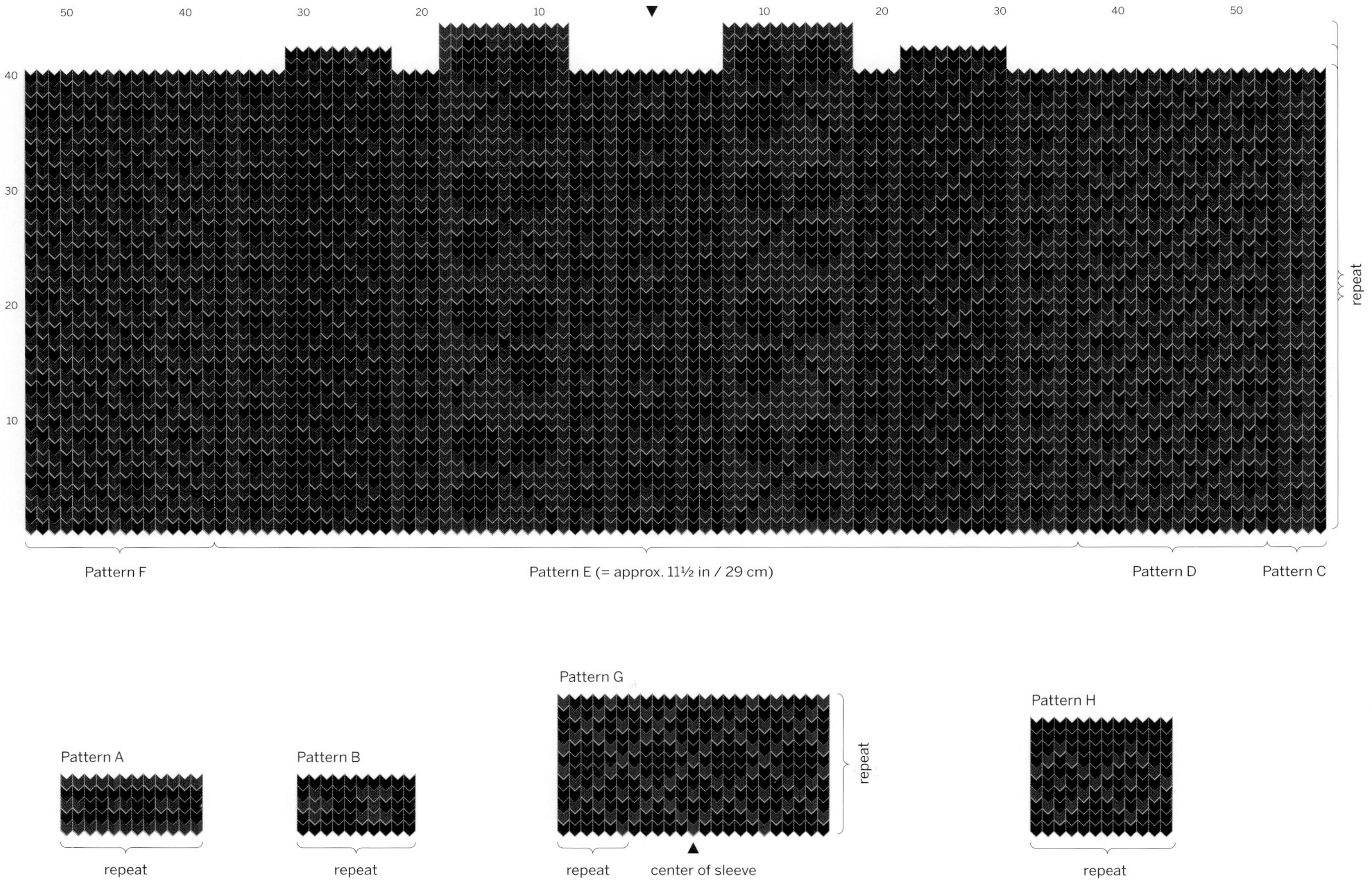

50
40
30
20
10
10
20
30
40
50
repeat
Pattern F
Pattern E (= approx. 11½ in / 29 cm)
Pattern D
Pattern C
Pattern A
repeat
Pattern B
repeat
Pattern G
repeat
repeat
center of sleeve
Pattern H
repeat

the center st of the split to determine where to begin the pattern. Increase 1 st with M1 at the beginning and end of the round with 2 sts between the increases approx. every ¾ (⅝-¾, ⅝) in / 2 (1.5-2, 1.5) cm 16 (18, 21) times = 87 (93, 101) sts. Work the new sts into pattern as well as possible. Continue until sleeve is given or desired length. BO 4 sts at the underarm = 83 (89, 97) sts rem. Now work back and forth in stockinette and pattern as est. *At the same time*, shape sleeve cap: BO 1 st on each side of every row 4 times, and then BO 1 st at each side on every other row 11 (13, 15) times. Next BO 1 st at each side of every row 8 times. End with BO 4 sts at the beginning of every row 3 times. BO rem 13 (15, 19) sts. Make the second sleeve the same way.

Sleeve Placket Edging

With smaller needles, and Color 1, pick up and knit about 12-13 sts per 2 in / 5 cm around edge of sleeve split = 1 knit row. Work 2 more rows in stockinette and then knit 1 row on WS = foldline + 3 more rows stockinette. BO on the next row. Work the split edging on the other sleeve cuff the same way. On each sleeve, turn facing under at foldline and sew down smoothly on WS.

Steek Finishing

Work two rows of machine stitching on each side of the 4 steek sts of armholes and, if worked in the round, the placket steek at center front. Carefully cut each steek open down center stitch. Seam shoulders.

Neckband

With larger circular and Color 2, pick up and knit approx. 94 (106, 118) sts around neck. The stitch count must be a multiple of 4+2. Work back and forth in Pattern A. The first and last sts of each row are edge sts and always knitted with Color 1. On the last row of Pattern A, adjust the stitch count to be a multiple of 6+5. Work Pattern H: K1 (edge st), 1 st Color 1, rep Pattern H until 2 sts rem, k1 Color 1, k1 (edge st). After completing Pattern H, knit 1 row on WS = foldline. Change to smaller circular and Color 2 and work in stockinette until the facing is same length as neckband to foldline. BO. Turn the facing to WS and sew down smoothly.

Edge along Front Placket and Neckband: With smaller circular and Color 1, pick up and knit approx. 12-13 sts per 2 in / 5 cm along one side of placket = 1 knit row. Work 2 more rows in stockinette, knit 1 row on WS (foldline) + 3 more rows in stockinette. BO on next row. Work the other side of the placket the same way. On each side, turn facing to WS and sew down smoothly. Sew short ends together neatly at center of placket. Seam shorts of band at top to neckband.

Finishing

Attach Sleeves

Pin each sleeve around armhole, centered at the shoulder seam and at underarm. Beginning at shoulder seam, sew down each side separately.

Sew 3 buttons on the right side of the front placket, evenly spaced down band. Make 3 button loops on opposite side of placket.

Right Sleeve: Sew 1 button on right side of split, approx. at middle. Make a button loop opposite.

Left Sleeve: As for right sleeve, but sew on button to left side of split.

Facing around Sleeve Top

For a finished look on the WS, you can knit a facing around the sleeve top to cover the cut edges around armhole. With smaller circular and your choice of color, pick up and knit approx. 13 sts per 2 in / 5 cm, from the center of underarm and all around the armhole. Work so that RS of facing will show on the outside when turned to cover the cut edges. Working back and forth, work 4 rows in stockinette and then BO loosely. Sew down facing on WS.

Weave in all ends neatly on WS.

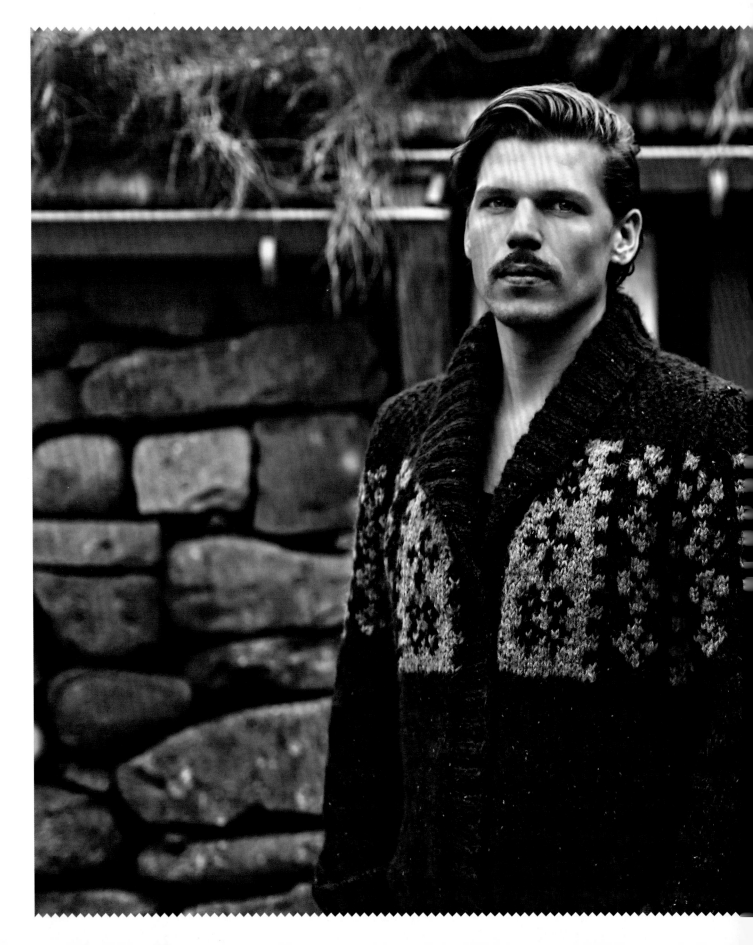

MEN'S NATIONAL COSTUME MOTIFS

These men's sweater motifs are used for men's jackets in traditional Faroese national costumes. The traditional hues were dark blue and light blue. Today these motifs are also used for other garments, in a variety of colors.

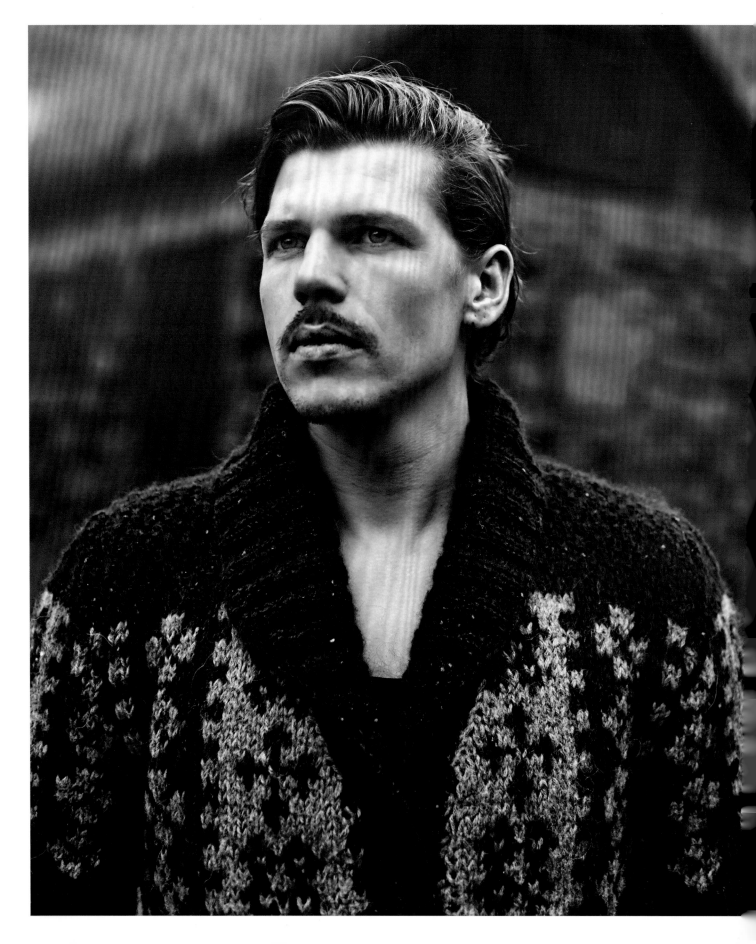

THE TAILOR

A soft men's cardigan with a shawl collar, knitted in Norwegian wool blended with tweed. Men's national costume motifs run across the chest and the shoulders feature texture knitting. This design was inspired by one of Tailor Debes's national costume jackets.

Sizes
Sweater: S (M, L, XL, XXL)

Finished Measurements
Chest: 37 (40¼, 43¼ 46½, 49¾) in / 94 (102, 110, 118, 126) cm
Length: 26 (26¾, 27½, 28¼, 29¼) in / 66 (68, 70, 72, 74) cm
Sleeve length: 18½ (19, 19¼, 19¾, 20) in / 47 (48, 49, 50, 51) cm or desired length
All measurements refer to the finished garment sizing and are calculated with the listed gauge.

Materials
Yarn:
CYCA #5 (bulky) Sandnes Garn Tweed (40% baby alpaca, 32% viscose, 20% nylon, 8% Merino wool, 164 yd/150 m / 50 g)
CYCA #3 (DK, light worsted) Sandnes Garn Smart (100% wool, 108 yd/99 m / 50 g)

Color Suggestions:
Color 1: Tweed: Navy Blue 5585 + Smart: Navy Blue 5575
Color 2: Tweed: Gray 1054 + Smart: Dark Gray Heather 1053

Yarn Amounts:
Color 1: Tweed: 250 (300, 350, 400, 450) g + Smart: 450 (500, 550, 600, 650) g
Color 2: Tweed: 50 (50, 100, 100, 100) g + Smart: 100 (100, 100, 100, 150) g

Notions
5 large press buttons

Needles
U.S. sizes 7, 8, and 9 / 4.5, 5, and 5.5 mm: Circulars and sets of 5 dpn

Gauge
15 sts stockinette on U.S. size 9 / 5.5 mm needles = 4 in / 10 cm
Adjust needle sizes to obtain correct gauge if necessary.

132

NOTES: If you knit single color stockinette more loosely than two-color pattern knitting, use needles one U.S. or one-half metric size smaller when working in stockinette.
Read through the entire pattern before you start to knit, because there are points at which several actions happen at the same time.

Front and Back
With Color 1 (= 1 strand of each yarn held together) and U.S. 7 / 4.5 mm circular, CO 132 (144, 156, 168, 180) sts. Work the ribbing back and forth as follows:
Row 1 (RS): K1 (edge st), (k2, p2) until 3 sts rem, end k2 + k1 (edge st).
Row 2 (WS): K1 (edge st), (p2, k2) until 3 sts rem, end p2 + k1 (edge st).

Rep Rows 1-2 until piece measures 2½ (2½, 2½, 2¾, 2¾) in / 6 (6, 6, 7, 7) cm. Now join to work in the rnd: at the end of a WS row, CO 4 sts for center front steek (see page 5). Steek sts are always worked in a single color and are not included in stitch counts. Change to U.S. 9 / 5.5 mm.
With Color 2 (1 strand of each yarn), work around in stockinette. On the first rnd, decrease 1 st at center of rnd = 131 (143, 155, 167, 179) sts rem. Pm at each side with 30 (33, 36, 39, 42) sts for each front and 71 (77, 83, 89, 95) sts for back.

Work around until piece measures 14¼ (14½, 15, 15½, 15¾) in / 36 (37, 38, 39, 40) cm. Now work Pattern A, beginning at the arrow for your size. When piece measures 17¼ (17¾, 18¼, 18½, 19) in / 44 (45, 46, 47, 48) cm, shape armhole at each side: BO 3 sts on each side of each side marker = 6 sts bound off at each side = 27 (30, 33, 36, 39) sts rem for each front and 65 (71, 77, 83, 89) sts for back. On the next rnd, CO 4 new sts over each gap. The 4 sts are the armhole steeks. Steek sts are always worked in a single color and are not included in stitch counts. On each side of each armhole steek, on

every other rnd, BO 2,1 (2,1; 2,1,1; 2,1,1; 2,1,1) sts. *At the same time*, when ¾ in / 2 cm above split of front and back, begin shaping V-neck: decrease 1 st on each side of the 4 center front steek sts on every other rnd 5 (5, 6, 8, 10) times and then decrease on every 4th rnd, 5 (6, 5, 5, 5) times = 14 (16, 18, 19, 20) sts rem for each front shoulder.
At the same time, after completing Pattern A, the rest of the body is worked with Color 1 and Pattern B. Continue until piece reaches total length after V-neck shaping. BO all sts.

Sleeves
With Color 1 (= 1 strand of each yarn held together) and U.S. 7 / 4.5 mm dpn, CO 40 (40, 44, 44, 48) sts. Divide sts onto dpn and join; pm for beginning of rnd. Work around in k2, p2 ribbing for 2½ (2½, 2½, 2¾, 2¾) in / 6 (6, 6, 7, 7) cm. Change to dpn U.S. 9 / 5.5 mm. Work around in stockinette with Color 1, increasing 1 st on the first rnd = 41 (41, 45, 45, 49) sts. Increase at underarm (K1, M1, knit to last st, M1, K1) about every 2¾ (2½, 2½, 1½, 2) in / 7 (6, 6, 4, 5) cm, 5 (6, 6, 8, 8) times = 51 (53, 57, 61, 65) sts.
At the same time, when sleeve measures 15 (15½, 15¾, 16¼, 16½) in / 38 (39, 40, 41, 42) cm, work Pattern A. Note the arrow for center of sleeve on the chart and count out to determine placement of 1st pattern st on sleeve. When sleeve measures given or desired length, ending on the same pattern row as for front and back, BO 6 sts centered at underarm = 45 (47, 51, 55, 59) sts rem. Continue with Pattern A, working back and forth, and, BO 2 sts at the beginning of every row once at each side. Next, decrease 1 st at the beginning of every row. When pattern is complete, continue with Color 1 and Pattern B. Decrease 1 st at each side a total of 12 (12, 13, 14, 14) times = 17 (19, 21, 23, 27) sts rem. BO 2 sts at the beginning of every row 2 times at each side. BO rem 9 (11, 13, 15, 19) sts. Make the other sleeve the same way.

Steek Finishing

Work two rows of machine stitching on each side of the 4 steek sts of armholes and at center front. Carefully cut each steek open down center stitch. Seam shoulders.

Front Bands and Collar

The band is worked in two parts, with each side worked separately and joined at back neck. With Color 2 (= 1 strand of each yarn held together), U.S. 7 / 4.5 mm circular, and RS facing, pick up and knit approx. 122 (126, 130, 134, 138) sts: begin at lower edge of right front, along the front edge, along V-neck, and to center of back neck. Pick up sts a bit more closely at the turn to the V-neck and along back neck so that the collar will be slightly fuller here. The stitch count must be a multiple of 4+2 sts. The first row is on the WS, beginning at center of back neck: work k2, p2 ribbing to end of row. Turn and work knit over knit and purl over purl. Continue in ribbing until collar measures 2½ in / 6 cm. On the next RS row, BO the sts from the lower edge up to the beginning of the V-neck. BO loosely in ribbing. Work to back neck. Begin shaping the collar just below the V-neck by working short rows: When 2 sts rem to base of V-neck, turn and slip the 1st st. Work back as est to center of back neck. On the next row, work until 4 sts rem; turn, sl 1st st, and work back to center of back neck. Continue the same way, with 2 sts fewer before each turn until the collar is approx. 6¼ in / 16 cm wide as measured at center of back neck. Work 1 complete row in ribbing on RS and then BO in ribbing on WS. Work the left side the same way, reversing shaping to match. Begin picking up sts at center back with RS facing.

Seam the collar neatly at center back neck.

Facing on Inside of Jacket

With 1 strand of Tweed Color 1 and circular U.S. 8 / 5 mm, pick up and knit approx. 15-16 sts per 4 in / 10 cm along the inside of the right side where the cut edge begins. Work 3 rows back and forth in stockinette and then BO. Work the facing for the left side the same way. Sew the facing neatly over the cut edges on the WS.

Attach Sleeves

Pin each sleeve around armhole, centered at the shoulder seam and at underarm. Beginning at shoulder seam, sew down each side separately.

Finishing

Gently steam press garment. Sew the press buttons to the right front, with the top one at the base of the V-neck, the bottom one centered on the ribbing, and with the rest evenly spaced in between.

Facing around Sleeve Top

For a finished look on the WS, you can knit a facing around the sleeve top to cover the cut edges around armhole. With U.S. 8 / 5 mm circular and one strand of Tweed, Color 1, pick up and knit approx. 8 sts per 2 in / 5 cm, from the center of underarm and all around the armhole. Work so that RS of facing will show on the outside when turned to cover the cut edges. Working back and forth, work 3 rows in stockinette and then BO loosely. Sew down facing on WS.

Weave in all ends neatly on WS.

133

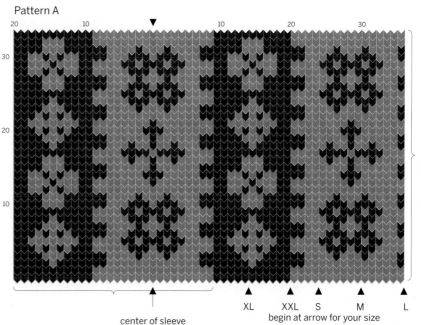

knit on RS, purl on WS
purl on RS, knit on WS

Pattern B

repeat

repeat

Color 1: Navy Blue + Navy Blue
Color 2: Gray + Dark Gray Heather

Pattern A

Approx. 7½ in / 19 cm

center of sleeve

XL   XXL   S   M   L
begin at arrow for your size

WOMEN'S NATIONAL COSTUME MOTIFS

These women's sweater motifs traditionally adorn the bodices of Faroese women's national costumes. These bodices were once knitted with up to four colors: red, blue, green, and white. Gradually, however, red and blue have become the hues of choice. Nowadays these motifs are also used in other garments, and in a variety of shades.

ANNA KATHRINA SÚSANNA

A short women's cardigan knitted in soft alpaca yarn. The women's national costume motifs decorate the body in the historical colors of red, blue, green, and white. This cardigan also features bands worked in seed stitch and hidden pockets with rolled edges. The design was inspired by Faroese national costume bodices, and by Tailor Debes's account of the beautiful and dignified matriarch of the wealthy á Látrinum farm.

Sizes
Sweater: S (M, L, XL)

Finished Measurements
Chest: 38¼ (40½, 43, 45¼) in / 97 (103, 109, 115) cm
Length: 22¾ (23¾, 24½, 25¼) in / 58 (60, 62, 64) cm
Sleeve length: 17¼ (17¾, 18¼, 18½) in / 44 (45, 46, 47) cm or desired length
All measurements refer to the finished garment sizing and are calculated with the listed gauge.

Materials
Yarn:
CYCA #1 (fingering) Sandnes Garn Mini Alpaca (100% alpaca, 164 yd/150 m / 50 g)

Color Suggestions:
Color 1: Navy Blue 5575
Color 2: Petroleum 7572
Color 3: Burgundy 4554
Color 4: Putty 1015

Yarn Amounts:
Color 1: 350 (400, 450, 500) g
Color 2: 50 (50, 50, 50) g
Color 3: 100 (100, 150, 150) g
Color 4: 50 (50, 50, 50) g

Notions
5 buttons

Needles
U.S. sizes 2.5 and possibly 4 / 3 and possibly 3.5 mm: Circulars and sets of 5 dpn

Gauge
27 sts and 26 rnds in pattern on larger needles = 4 in / 10 cm
Adjust needle sizes to obtain correct gauge if necessary.

NOTE: If you knit single color stockinette more loosely than two-color pattern knitting, use needles one U.S. or one-half metric size smaller when working in stockinette.

SEED STITCH
Row 1: (K1, p1) across.
Row 2 and all subsequent rows: Work purl over knit and knit over purl.

Front and Back
With Color 1 and U.S. 2.5 / 3 mm circular, CO 267 (283, 299, 315) sts. Work back and forth as follows:

Row 1 (WS): Work in seed st over the first 6 sts (= edge sts), knit until 6 sts rem, work 6 sts in seed st (= edge sts).
Row 2 (RS): Work in seed st over the first 6 sts (= edge sts), knit until 6 sts rem, work 6 sts in seed st (= edge sts).
Rows 3-4: Work as for Rows 1-2.

Now work in seed st over the first and last 6 sts of each row for the edge sts and in stockinette for rem sts. Work back and forth until piece measures 2½ in / 6 cm. Place edge sts on holders to be worked during finishing. At the end of WS row, CO 4 sts for center front steek (see page 5). Steek sts are always worked in a single color and are not included in stitch counts. Change, if necessary for gauge, to U.S. 4 / 3.5 mm circular and begin working in the round; pm for beginning of rnd. Work around in stockinette and Pattern A. Begin and end at the arrow for your size.

Work as est until piece measures 5½ (6, 6¼, 6¾) in / 14 (15, 16, 17) cm. On the next rnd, use a smooth contrast-color waste yarn to knit the sts for the pocket: Knit the first 15 (17, 18, 20) sts in pattern, knit the next 32 (32, 34, 34) sts with the waste yarn. slide the

pocket sts back to left needle and knit them in pattern with working yarn. Work around until 47 (49, 52, 54) sts rem. Work 32 (32, 34, 34) pocket sts as before and then work rem sts in pattern.

Continue around in pattern as est until piece measures 15½ (15¾, 16¼, 16½) in / 39 (40, 41, 42) cm. BO each side st + 4 sts at each side of each side st = 9 sts bound off at each side. On the next rnd, CO 4 new sts over each gap for the armhole steeks. Continue around in Pattern A and, *at the same time*, shape armholes: at each side of each armhole steek, on every other rnd, BO 3,2,2,1,1,1 (3,2,2,2,1,1; 3,2,2,2,1,1,1; 3,2,2,2,2,1,1,1) sts. Work without further shaping until piece measures 3½ (4, 4, 4¼) in / 9 (10,10, 11) cm from underarm. BO the 4 steek sts at center front for the neck + 5 (6, 7, 8) sts on each side of the steek. Work each side separately and decrease at the neck at the beginning of every row: BO 4,3,2,2,1,1,1,1,1,1 sts (all sizes) = 26 (28, 30, 32) sts rem for each shoulder. *At the same time*, when body is ¾ in / 2 cm less than total length, BO the center back 43 (45, 47, 49) sts for back neck. Work each side separately. At back neck, on every other row, BO 2,1 sts (all sizes) = 26 (28, 30, 32) sts rem for each shoulder. *At the same time*, when piece is ⅜ in / 1 cm less than total length, work Pattern B. It will look best if you finish Pattern A after a complete block in the pattern. Adjust the beginning of Pattern B so that the burgundy "stripes" will align directly over each other when the shoulders are joined.

After completing Pattern B, BO with Color 1. Work the other side the same way, reversing shaping to match.

Sleeves

With Color 1 and U.S. 2.5 / 3 mm dpn, CO 54 (56, 58, 60) sts. Divide sts onto dpn and join, being careful not to twist cast-on row. Pm for beginning of rnd. Purl 1 rnd, knit 1 rnd, purl 1 rnd = 2 ridges as at bottom edge of body. Continue around in stockinette. Approx. every ¾ (¾, ¾, ⅝) in / 2 (2, 2, 1.5) cm, increase as follows: K1, M1, knit until 1 st rem, M1, k1. Work the increase rnd a total of 18 (20, 22, 24) times = 90 (96, 102, 108) sts. *At the same time*, when sleeve measures 2 in / 5 cm, make 2 more garter ridges as for sleeve edge. Continue around in stockinette and increases until sleeve measures given or desired length. BO 8 sts centered at underarm. Now work back and forth. At beginning of every row BO 2,2 sts for all sizes. Next, decrease 1 st at the beginning of every row until 30 (32, 34, 36) sts rem. At the beginning of every row BO 2,2,2 sts (all sizes). BO rem sts. Make the other sleeve the same way.

Steek Finishing

Gently steam press garment. Work two rows of machine stitching on each side of the 4 steek sts of armholes and at center front. Carefully cut each steek open down center stitch. Seam shoulders. Weave in all ends neatly on WS.

■ Color 1: Navy Blue
■ Color 2: Petroleum
■ Color 3: Burgundy
□ Color 4: Putty

Pattern B

repeat

Pattern A

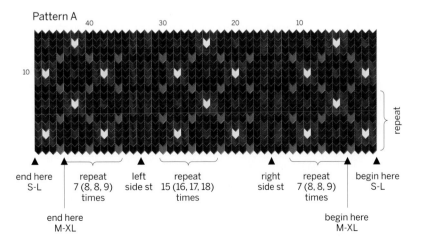

end here
S-L

end here
M-XL

repeat
7 (8, 8, 9)
times

left
side st

repeat
15 (16, 17, 18)
times

right
side st

repeat
7 (8, 8, 9)
times

begin here
M-XL

begin here
S-L

repeat

Finishing

Left Front Band
Place the held sts of left front band onto U.S. 2.5 / 3 mm needles. CO 3 new sts at the side next to body. These 3 sts are the facing that will be sewn over the cut edges. Purl these sts on RS and knit on WS so that the stockinette side will face up when you sew the facing over the cut edges.

NOTE: So that the front band won't be shorter than the facing and draw in, about every 10 rows, work 2 extra rows over the seed sts only = short rows.
Continue in seed st over the 6 outermost sts and reverse stockinette over the facing until the band reaches the neck without stretching. It is better to make the band a little too long rather than too short so you don't have to add rows when sewing the facing to the jacket.

BO the 3 facing sts and place the rem 6 sts on a holder.
Mark placement for the buttons: the top one about 4¾ in / 12 cm down from neck and the bottom one about 5½-6 in / 14-15 cm up from the bottom edge, with the rest spaced evenly between.

Right Front Band
Work as for left front band but reverse image and with buttonholes spaced as for button placement.

Work each buttonhole over 2 sts, 2 sts in from the front edge.

Sew the front bands neatly to front edges.

Fold facing over cut edges and sew down on WS.

Neckband
Slip the sts of right front band onto U.S. 2.5 / 3 mm circular and attach Color 1. Pick up and knit approx. 13-14 sts per 2 in / 5 cm along neck edge and then slip the left front band sts to needle and knit = 1st RS row. Work back and forth in seed st until neckband measures approx. ¾ in / 2 cm. BO rather loosely in seed st.

Pockets
Insert a dpn U.S. 2.5 / 3 mm through the sts below waste yarn and another dpn through sts above waste yarn. Carefully remove waste yarn. Divide the sts onto 4 dpn and pick up and knit 1 extra st at each side to avoid holes. With Color 1, join and work the 1st two rnds as follows:
Rnd 1: Knit all the sts around.
Rnd 2: Purl over the sts from the bottom edge (= 1 ridge) and knit the rem sts.

Now work around in stockinette for about 4¾ in / 12 cm. BO. Sew down the pocket at lower edge.

Rolled Edge for Pocket Opening
With Color 1 and dpn U.S. 2.5 / 3 mm, pick up and knit sts along the lower edge of pocket opening. Work back and forth in stockinette with RS facing, for about ⅝ in / 1.5 cm. BO. The wrong side will roll forward. Sew the short ends of the rolled edge to the jacket.

Attach Sleeves
Pin each sleeve around armhole, centered at the shoulder seam and at underarm. Beginning at shoulder seam, sew down each side separately.

Facing around Sleeve Top
For a finished look on the WS, you can knit a facing around the sleeve top to cover the cut edges around the armholes. With U.S. 2.5 / 3 mm circular and Color 1, pick up and knit approx. 13-14 sts per 2 in / 5 cm, from the center of underarm and all around the armhole. Work so that RS of facing will show on the outside when turned to cover the cut edges. Working back and forth, work 4 rows in stockinette and then BO loosely. Sew down facing on WS.

Sew on buttons.

Weave in all ends neatly on WS.

BEINTA

A short women's cardigan with buttons, knitted in fine Norwegian wool. My grandmother knitted a cardigan with this design long before I was born. All the girls in our family took to it, and the cardigan's very well-worn after all these years! This is my grandmother's four-colored take on the women's national costume motif, called *áttablaðsrósa í rútarum*—"eight-petaled rose in diamond trellis."

Sizes
S (M, L, XL)

Finished Measurements
Chest: 37 (39¾, 42½, 45) in / 94 (101, 108, 114) cm
Length: 24½ (25¼, 26, 26¾) in / 62 (64, 66, 68) cm
Sleeve length: 18½ (19, 19¼, 19¾) in / 47 (48, 49, 50) cm or desired length.
All measurements refer to the finished garment sizing and are calculated with the listed gauge.

Materials
Yarn:
CYCA #2 (sport, baby) Sandnes Garn Tove (100% Norwegian wool, 175 yd/160 m / 50 g)

Color Suggestions:
Version 1:
Color 1: Light Gray Heather 1035
Color 2: Natural 1012
Color 3: Charcoal Heather 1088
Color 4: Dark Gray Heather 1053

Version 2:
Color 1: Natural Heather 2641
Color 2: Dark Blue 6364
Color 3: Navy Blue 5575
Color 4: Corn Yellow 2015

Yarn Amounts:
Color 1: 200 (200, 250, 250) g
Color 2: 100 (100, 150, 150) g
Color 3: 150 (150, 200, 200, 50) g
Color 4: 50 (50, 50, 50) g

Notions
8 (8, 9, 9) buttons

Needles
U.S. sizes 2.5 and 4 / 3 and 3.5 mm: circulars and sets of 5 dpn

Gauge
24 sts in stockinette on larger needles = 4 in / 10 cm
Adjust needle sizes to obtain correct gauge if necessary.

Front and Back
With Color 1 and smaller circular, CO 232 (248, 264, 280) sts. Work back and forth as follows:
Row 1 (WS): K1 (edge st), (p2, k2) to last 3 sts, end p2, k1 (edge st).
Row 2 (RS): K1 (edge st), (k2, p2) to last 3 sts, end k2, k1 (edge st).
Rep these two rows, always keeping the first and last sts as knit sts. *At the same time*, work the following stripe sequence:
3 rows Color 3
3 rows Color 1
3 rows Color 4
3 rows Color 3
3 rows Color 1
3 rows Color 2

The sweater will now be worked in the round: At the end of WS row, CO 4 sts for center front steek (see page 5). Steek sts are always worked in a single color and are not included in stitch counts. Change to larger circular and Color 2. On the first rnd, knit, decreasing 15 sts (all sizes) evenly spaced around. It will look best if you decrease over the purl columns of the ribbing = 217 (233, 249, 265) sts + the 4 steek sts rem. Pm at each side with 113 (121, 129, 137) sts for the back and 104 (112, 120, 128) sts for the front. Continue around in stockinette and Pattern A, beginning and ending at the arrow for your size. Work as est until piece measures approx. 2½ (2½, 2¾, 2¾) in / 6 (6, 7, 7) cm less than given length and then BO the 4 steek sts + 5 (6, 7, 8) sts on each side of the steek for the neck. Continue back and forth in pattern and, at neck edge, at the beginning of each row, BO 4,3,2,1,1 (4,3,2,2,1; 4,3,2,2,1,1; 5,3,2,2,1,1) sts. When piece is approx. ¾ in / 2 cm less than total length, BO the center back 17 (19, 21, 23) sts for back neck. Work each side separately. At back neck, on every other row, BO 10,2 (11,2; 12,2; 13,2) sts. *At the same time*, when piece is ⅜ in / 1 cm less than total length, end with a pattern row on the WS

and change to Color 3. Knit 4 rows = 2 ridges. BO rem sts. Each shoulder on front/back now has 36 (38, 40, 42) sts. Work the other side the same way, reversing shaping to match.

Sleeves
With Color 3 and smaller dpn, CO 48 (48, 52, 52) sts. Divide sts onto dpn and join, being careful not to twist cast-on row. Pm for beginning of rnd. Work around in k2, p 2 ribbing in the same color sequence as for the body. Change to larger dpn. Knit 1 rnd with Color 2, increasing 6 (8, 8, 10) sts evenly spaced around = 54 (56, 60, 62) sts. Continue around in stockinette and Pattern A. Note the arrow for center of sleeve and count out to the side to determine where to start the pattern. Approx. every ⅝ in / 1.5 cm (all sizes), increase as follows: K1, M1, knit until 1 st rem, M1, k1. Work the increase rnd a total of 26 (28, 28, 29) times = 106 (112, 116, 120) sts. Continue around in pattern with increases worked into pattern as neatly as possible until sleeve measures given or desired length. It will look best if you end the pattern after either a whole or half "flower." Knit 1 rnd with Color 1 only. Turn the sleeve inside out and work 5 rows back and forth in stockinette for the facing. Loosely BO knitwise. Make the other sleeve the same way.

Steek Finishing
Gently steam press garment.
Work two rows of machine stitching on each side of the 4 steek sts at center front. Carefully cut steek open down center stitch.

Measure top of sleeve and then measure down from shoulder to determine depth of armhole. Work two rows of machine stitching on each side of the center st of armhole. Carefully cut each steek open down center stitch.

Seam shoulders.

Left Front Band

Tip: At the beginning of every other row at the edge: each time you begin to work a new row, from and including the 2nd row, bring the yarn to the front/ towards you. Slip the first st and then move the yarn back between the 1st and 2nd sts. Continue as explained below. This way, you have a smooth edge on the outer side of the front.

With Color 3 and smaller needles, CO 11 sts. Work back and forth. Throughout, knit the 8 outermost sts in garter st for front band and work the inner 3 sts in reverse stockinette: purl on RS and knit on WS for facing to be folded over the cut edges.

Work band until it reaches the neck bind-off without stretching. Make sure it is not too long or it will ruffle. It is better to have it a little too long rather than too short so you don't have to add more rows when sewing to the jacket.

NOTE: So that the front band won't be shorter than the facing and draw in, about every 12 rows, work 2 extra rows

over the garter st only = short rows.

BO the 3 facing sts and place the rem 8 sts on a holder.

Mark the placement of 8 (8, 9, 9) buttons on the band: the top one will be centered on the neckband which is worked last; place the bottom one about ¾ in / 2 cm up from the bottom edge, and the rest spaced evenly between.

Right Front Band

Work as for the left front band, reversing garter st and facing sts, and adding buttonholes. Each buttonhole is worked over 2 sts, 3 sts in from the edge. Space buttonholes as for buttons. *Buttonhole:* BO 2 sts and, on following row, CO 2 sts over the gap.
When both bands are finished, sew the garter st edges to the front edges of body. Sew the facings over the cut edges on WS.

Neckband

Slip the held sts of right front band to smaller circular. With Color 3, knit front band sts, pick up and knit approx.

94 (98, 102, 106) sts around the neck and then place and knit the sts of left front band onto circular = 110 (114, 118, 122) sts total. The stitch count must be a multiple of 4+2 sts. Work back and forth in k2, p2 ribbing, ending with k2. *At the same time,* work in this color sequence:
3 rows Color 3
3 rows Color 4
3 rows Color 1
3 rows Color 3.

NOTE: Don't forget to work the top buttonhole centered on the right side. Work as for previous buttonholes but work it 4 sts in from the edge (= centered over a k2 column in ribbing).

BO loosely in ribbing.

Attach Sleeves

Pin each sleeve around armhole, centered at the shoulder seam and at underarm. Beginning at shoulder seam, sew down each side separately, sewing inside the facing. Sew down the facing on WS, over the cut edges.

Sew on buttons. Weave in all ends neatly on WS.

149

Color 1: Natural Heather	
Color 2: Dark Blue	
Color 3: Navy Blue	
Color 4: Corn Yellow	

Pattern A

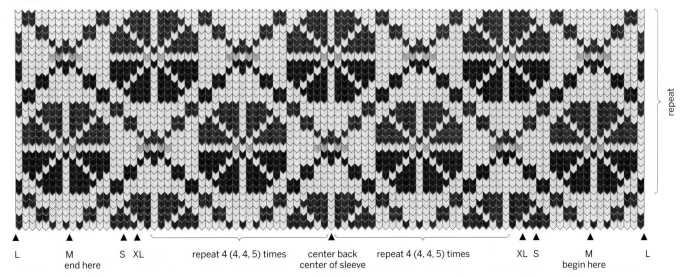

L   M   S XL   repeat 4 (4, 4, 5) times   center back   repeat 4 (4, 4, 5) times   XL S   M   L
     end here   center of sleeve   begin here

repeat

RAKUL

A knee-length women's sweater longer at the back than in the front, knitted in silk-mohair with the pattern in tweed. Half of the body is adorned with the women's national costume motif (*áttablaðsstjørna í rútarum*—"eight-pointed star in diamond trellis").

At the Faroese National History Museum in Tórshavn, a short-sleeved red sweater with the pattern *áttablaðsstjørna í rútarum*—"eight-pointed star in diamond trellis"—is on display. The motif resembles those on the so-called "silk nightshirts" exhibited at several Norwegian museums. These exquisite garments, knitted in silk with purl stitch patterns, were often richly embellished with gold or silver embroidery on the chest and sleeves. Nobody knows for certain where the garments came from, but they were probably produced at professional knitting workshops in Europe in the 17th century. The sweaters that were later knitted in wool with the same motif were probably based on these silk nightshirts.

Sizes
Sweater: S (M, L, XL)

Finished Measurements
Chest: 43¼ (47¼, 51¼, 55¼) in / 110 (120, 130, 140) cm
Length, back: 35 (36¼, 37½, 38½) in / 89 (92, 95, 98) cm
Length, front: 30¾ (31½, 32¾, 33½) in / 78 (80, 83, 85) cm
Sleeve length: 18½ (19, 19¼, 19¾) in / 47 (48, 49, 50) cm or desired length
All measurements refer to the finished garment sizing and are calculated with the listed gauge.

Materials
Yarn:
CYCA #4 (worsted, afghan, Aran) Sandnes Garn Silk Mohair (60% kid mohair, 25% silk, 15% wool, 306 yd/280 m / 50 g)
CYCA #5 (bulky) Sandnes Garn Tweed (40% baby alpaca, 32% viscose, 20% nylon, 8% Merino wool, 164 yd/150 m / 50 g)

Color Suggestions:
Version 1:
Color 1: Silk Mohair: Deep Blue 6081 + Silk Mohair: Moss Green 9573
Color 2: Tweed: Navy Blue 5585

Version 2:
Color 1: Silk Mohair: Natural 1012 + Silk Mohair: Light Gray Heather 1032
Color 2: Tweed: Charcoal 1087

Yarn Amounts:
Color 1: Silk Mohair: 150 (150, 150, 200) g of each color
Color 2: Tweed: 150 (200, 200, 250) g

Needles
U.S. sizes 7 and 10 / 4.5 and 6 mm: Circulars and sets of 5 dpn

Gauge
14 sts in pattern on larger needles = 4 in / 10 cm
Adjust needle sizes to obtain correct gauge if necessary.

NOTE: If you knit single color stockinette more loosely than two-color pattern knitting, use needles one U.S. or one-half metric size smaller when working in stockinette.

Front and Back
With Color 1 (= 1 strand of each color held together) and smaller circular, CO 152 (168, 184, 200) sts. Join, being careful not to twist cast-on row. Pm for beginning of rnd.

Work around in k2, p2 ribbing for 3¼ in / 8 cm (all sizes). Change to larger circular. Pm at each side with 76 (84, 92, 100) sts each for front and back. Knit 3 rnds in stockinette. On the next rnd, begin short rows for back to lengthen it. Work around until 1 st rem before 2nd marker. Bring yarn to front (RS), sl next st, move yarn to WS and slip st back to left needle; turn. Purl back over all sts until 1 st rem before opposite marker (= beginning of rnd). Sl next st, bring yarn to front (WS) and slip st back to left needle; turn. Knit 3 rounds over all sts, but, when you come to the wrap around the slipped st at a turn, work it as: insert right needle down into the front loop of the wrap, bring up the loop/stitch and lay it behind the next st on left needle. Work the sts together as a twisted knit (= through back loops). **NOTE:** It is important that the yarn/loop that will be worked together with the st on the next rnd not be too tight.

Repeat the short rows on every 4th rnd until the back is approx. 4¼ (4¾, 4¾, 5¼) in / 11 (12, 12, 13) cm longer than the front.

Continue around in stockinette until the piece measures 9½ (9¾, 10¾, 11) in / 24 (25, 27, 28) cm at center front. The rest of the body will be worked in Pattern A as follows: *Pm around the

1st st = side st, k1 with Color 1 (= edge st), k1 Color 2, k1 Color 1, k1 Color 2. Work as shown on the chart over the next 69 (77, 85, 93) sts, beginning and ending at each side as indicated by the arrows for your size. End with k1 Color 2, k1 Color 1, k1 Color 2*. Rep * to * once more. There will be 7 vertical stripes on each side. The center of these 7 sts at each side is the side st.

Continue around as est until piece measures 22 (22½, 22¾, 23¼) in / 56 (57, 58, 59) cm at center front. From now on, the 7 sts at each side will be worked in Pattern A to avoid stripes up along the sleeves when the sweater is finished. It will look best with the star pattern. Work as now est until piece measures 27½ (28¼, 29¼, 30) in / 70 (72, 74, 76) cm at center front. Count out from the center st at center front and then BO 8 (9, 10, 11) sts on each side of center st = 17 (19, 21, 23) sts bound off for neck. Now work back and forth in pattern and, *at the same time*, at beginning of every row at neck edge BO 2,1,1,1,1 sts (all sizes). Continue until body is given total length. BO all sts. There is no shaping for the back neck.

Sleeves
With Color 2 (= 1 strand of each color held together) and smaller dpn, CO 36 (36, 40, 40) sts. Divide sts onto dpn and join. Work around in k2, p2 ribbing for 2½ in / 6 cm. Change to larger dpn. Work around in Pattern A as follows: Pm around the 7 center sts of underarm. These sts are worked throughout as: knit 1 st each Color 2, Color 1, Color 2, Color 1, Color 2, Color 1, Color 2. This makes 7 vertical stripes on the underside of the sleeve. The center of the 7 sts is the center st of underarm. Note the arrow for the center of sleeve on Pattern A and count out to determine where to begin the pattern.

To shape sleeve, increase with M1 on each side of the outermost stripe in Color 2 so that there are always 7 sts between increases at underarm. Work the new sts into pattern as well as possible. Work increases as described above approx. every 1¼ (2, 2, 2) in / 3 (2.5, 2.5, 2.5) cm a total of 13 (15, 15, 17) times = 62 (66, 70, 74) sts. Continue until sleeve reaches given or desired length. Knit 1 rnd with Color 1 after the last rnd of the pattern. Turn sleeve inside out and work 3 rows back and forth in stockinette for the facing. Loosely BO knitwise. Make the other sleeve the same way.

Finishing

NOTE: The back and the front are 1 st off in relation to each other because of the side sts. Make sure to sew the seams so that the pattern is symmetrical on both sides of the armholes when finishing.

Steek Finishing

Gently steam press garment. Measure top of sleeve and then measure down from shoulder to determine depth of armhole. Work two rows of machine stitching on each side of the center st of armhole. Carefully cut each steek open down center stitch.

Neckband

With Color 1 (1 strand of each color held together) and smaller circular, pick up and knit approx. 80 (84, 88, 92) sts around neck. The stitch count must be a multiple of 4. Join, pm for beginning of rnd, and work around in k2, p2 ribbing for 12¾ in / 32 cm. BO in ribbing.

Attach Sleeves

Pin each sleeve around armhole, centered at the shoulder seam and at underarm. Beginning at shoulder seam, sew down each side separately, sewing inside the facing. Sew down the facing on WS, over the cut edges.

Weave in all ends neatly on WS.

Color 1: Deep Blue + Moss Green
Color 2: Navy Blue

Pattern A

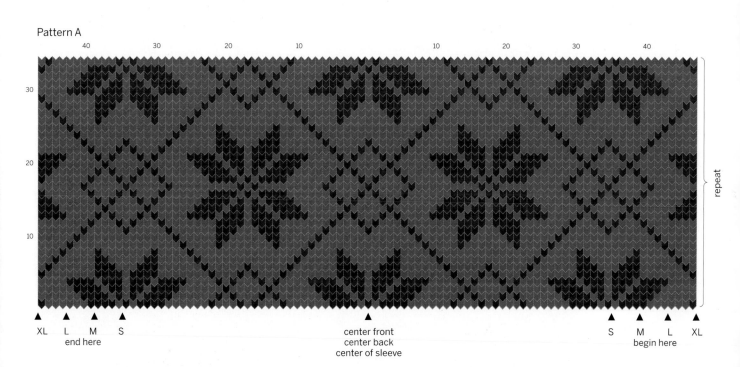

XL L M S   center front / center back / center of sleeve   S M L XL
end here   begin here

ANNA MARIA

A gossamer women's sweater with puff
sleeves, knitted in a single silk-mohair yarn
with a national costume motif in tweed.
The design was inspired by Tailor Debes's
story about the daughter of Jóannes the
Wise, who returned to her home village
after working in the capital city. She was
considered a bit of a fashionista because
she wore high wooden shoes and sweaters
with tucks at the shoulders.

161

Sizes
Sweater: S (M, L, XL)

Finished Measurements
Chest: 35½ (37¾, 40¼, 42½) in /
90 (96, 102, 108) cm
Length: 21¼ (21¾, 22, 22½) in /
54 (55, 56, 57) cm
Sleeve length: 18½ (19, 19¼, 19¾)
in / 47 (48, 49, 50) cm or desired
length
All measurements refer to the
finished garment sizing and are
calculated with the listed gauge.

Materials
Yarn:
CYCA #4 (worsted, afghan, Aran)
Sandnes Garn Silk Mohair (60%
kid mohair, 25% silk, 15% wool, 306
yd/280 m / 50 g)
CYCA #5 (bulky) Sandnes Garn
Tweed (40% baby alpaca, 32%
viscose, 20% nylon, 8% Merino
wool, 164 yd/150 m / 50 g)

Color Suggestions:
Version 1:
Color 1: Silk Mohair: Strawberry
Red 4065
Color 2: Tweed: Navy Blue 5585

Version 2:
Color 1: Silk Mohair: Acid Yellow
2005
Color 2: Tweed: Black 1100

Yarn Amounts:
Color 1: Silk Mohair: 100 (100, 150,
150) g
Color 2: Tweed: 150 (200, 200,
250) g

Needles
U.S. sizes 2.5 and 6 / 3 and 4 mm:
Circulars and sets of 5 dpn

Gauge
20 sts and 22 rnds in pattern on
larger needles = 4 in / 10 cm
Adjust needle sizes to obtain
correct gauge if necessary.

162

Front and Back
With Color 1 and smaller circular,
CO 180 (192, 204, 216) sts. Join, being
careful not to twist cast-on row. Pm for
beginning of rnd. Work around in k2,
p2 ribbing for 2¾ in / 7 cm (all sizes).
Change to larger circular. Pm at each
side with 90 (96, 102, 108) sts each
for front and back. Now work around
in stockinette and charted pattern
as follows: *K1 Color 2, k1 Color 1,
k1 Color 2. Work Pattern A over the
next 87 (93, 99, 105) sts, beginning and
ending at each side at arrow for your
size*. Rep from * to * once more. Work
as est until piece measures 13¾ (13¾,
14¼, 14¼) in / 35 (35, 36, 36) cm.
Shape Armholes: At each side, BO 4 (4,
5, 5) sts after marker and 1 (1, 2, 2) sts
before marker = 5 (5, 7, 7) sts bound off
centered over the stripes at each side
and 85 (91, 95, 101) sts rem each for
front and back. Now work each part
separately.

Back
Work back and forth in Pattern A
as before and continue to shape
armholes: at the beginning of each
row, BO 2,1,1 (2,1,1,1; 2,1,1,1; 2,2,1,1) sts
= 77 (81, 85, 89) sts rem. Work without
further shaping until piece measures
21 (21¼, 21¾, 22) in / 53 (54, 55, 56)
cm. BO the center 45 (47, 49, 51) sts
for the back neck and work each side
separately. At back neck edge, on every
other row, BO 1,1 sts (all sizes). When
piece measures total length, BO the
rem 14 (15, 16, 17) sts for the shoulder.
Work the other side the same way,
reversing shaping to match.

Front
Work as for back, shaping armholes
the same way. When piece measures
19¾ (20, 20½, 21) in / 50 (51, 52, 53)
cm, BO the center 35 (37, 39, 41) sts
for the neck and then work each side
separately. At neck edge, on every
other row, BO 3,2,1,1 sts (all sizes).
Continue until front is same length as
back and then BO rem 14 (15, 16, 17) sts

for shoulder. Work the other side the
same way, reversing shaping to match.

Sleeves
NOTE: Read through this entire
section before you start to knit because
there are points at which several
actions happen at the same time.

With Color 1 and smaller dpn, CO
40 (40, 44, 44) sts. Divide sts onto
dpn and join. Work around in k2, p2
ribbing for 4¼ in / 11 cm (all sizes).
Change to larger dpn and continue
around in stockinette and Pattern A
as follows: Pm around the 3 center
sts at underarm. These 3 sts will be
worked throughout as: k1 Color 2, k1
Color 1, k1, Color 2 = 3 vertical stripes
up from the underarm. The center
of these 3 stripe sts is the center of
the underarm. Note arrow on chart
indicating the center of the sleeve.
Count out to determine where to begin
the rnd. Also note the arrow at the left
side of the chart which indicates how
to begin the first rnd after the ribbing.
This ensures that the pattern will end
at the same place on the body before
the armholes.

Shape Sleeve: Increase with M1 on
each side of the outermost stripes in
Color 2 at underarm = 3 sts between
the increases throughout. Work new
sts into pattern as well as possible.

Work the increases every ¾ (¾, ¾,
⅝-¾) in / 2 (2, 2, 1.5-2) cm. Increase
a total of 16 (18, 18, 20) times = 72 (76,
80, 84) sts. Work as est until sleeve
measures given or desired length,
ending at the same place as for the
body. Now work back and forth in
Pattern A, shaping sleeve cap. At the
beginning of every row, BO 3,2,1,1
(3,2,1,1,1; 4,2,1,1,1; 4,2,2,1,1) sts = 58 (60,
62, 64) sts rem. Continue until sleeve
is 6¼ (6¾, 7, 7) in / 16 (17, 18, 18) cm
long. On the next RS row, *Sl 1, k2tog,
psso*. Rep * to * across row. BO the
rem sts on the next row.

Make the other sleeve the same way.

Finishing
Gently steam press garment. Seam
shoulders.

Neckband
With Color 2 and larger circular, pick
up and knit approx. 72 (76, 76, 80)
sts around neck. The stitch count
must be a multiple of 4. Join, pm for
beginning of rnd, and work around in
k2, p2 ribbing for about 1¾ in / 4.5 cm.
Loosely BO in ribbing.

Attach Sleeves
Pin each sleeve around armhole,
centered at the shoulder seam and
at underarm. Beginning at shoulder
seam, sew down each side separately.

Weave in all ends neatly on WS.

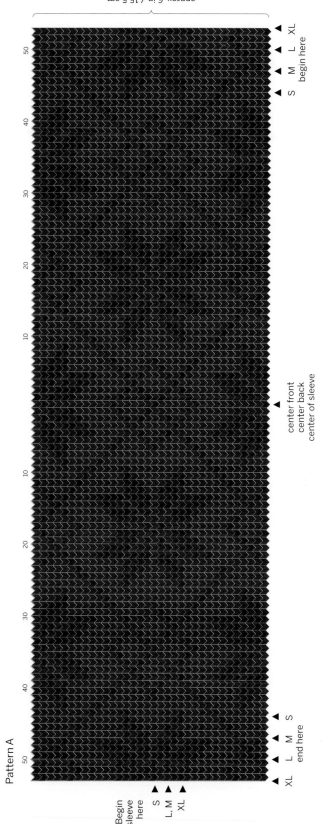

approx. 6 in / 15.5 cm
repeat

Color 1: Strawberry Red
Color 2: Navy Blue

Pattern A

163

JOSEFINA

A short women's cardigan, closed with buttons and knitted in Norwegian wool. This design combines women's national costume motifs and a rose panel worked with silk-mohair. It was inspired by one of Tailor Debes's stories about a young woman from the provinces who visited a haberdashery in the capital to buy fabric for a bonnet.

"As was customary, not only on the Faroe Islands but in all the Nordic countries, in church men sat on the right side and women on the left side, and so each set of pews was referred to as the men's side or the women's side. It was said that women would make sure they wore their best finery on their right, so if their beloved sat on the other side and looked over, they would see this 'best' side. On St. Olaf's Day (July 29th), a girl from another village came into Mettustova to buy fabric for a bonnet and Josefina was going to cut it. But this fabric had such a large pattern that only one repeat of its central feature, a rose, could fit on a bonnet. Some wanted to have the rose on the back of the bonnet, while others wanted it centered at the top of the head.

Josefina asked in her Tórshavn dialect: 'Where would you like your rose?'

The girl looked down and thought about it. Suddenly, she looked up and said: 'It should be placed on the men's side!'"

Excerpt from the story "Mettustova" in *Tales of the Old Days*
by Hans M. Debes, 1977

Sizes
Sweater: S (M, L, XL)

Finished Measurements
Chest: 34 (38¼, 42½, 47) in / 86 (97, 108, 119) cm
Length: approx. 22¾ (23¾, 24½, 25¼) in / 58 (60, 62, 64) cm
Sleeve length: 17¾ (18¼, 18½, 19¼) in / 45 (46, 47, 49) cm or desired length
All measurements refer to the finished garment sizing and are calculated with the listed gauge.

Materials
Yarn:
CYCA #3 (DK, light worsted)
Sandnes Garn Smart (100% wool, 108 yd/99 m / 50 g)
CYCA #4 (worsted, afghan, Aran)
Sandnes Garn Silk Mohair (60% kid mohair, 25% silk, 15% wool, 306 yd/280 m / 50 g)

Color Suggestions:
Smart:
Color 1: Black 1099
Color 2: Green 8264
Color 3: Dusty Green 7243
Color 4: Natural 1012
Silk Mohair:
Color 5: Burgundy 4545 + Strawberry Red 4065

Yarn Amounts:
Smart:
Color 1: 350 (400, 400, 450) g
Color 2: 50 (50, 100, 100) g
Color 3: 200 (200, 250, 300) g
Color 4: 150 (150, 200, 250) g
Silk Mohair:
Color 5: 50 g of each color—all sizes

Notions
8 buttons

Needles
U.S. sizes 4 and 6 / 3.5 and 4 mm: Circulars and sets of 5 dpn

Gauge
22 sts and 27 rnds in pattern on larger needles = 4 in / 10 cm
Adjust needle sizes to obtain correct gauge if necessary.

NOTES: If you knit single color stockinette more loosely than two-color pattern knitting, use needles one U.S. or one-half metric size smaller when working in stockinette.

Front and Back
With Color 1 and smaller circular, CO 180 (204, 228, 252) sts. Work back and forth as follows:
Row 1 (WS): K1 (edge st, (p2, k2) until 3 sts rem and end with p2, k1 (edge st).
Row 2 (RS): K1 (edge st, (k2, p2) until 3 sts rem and end with k2, k1 (edge st). Rep these 2 rows until piece measures approx. 1½ in / 4 cm. CO 4 sts at the end of the last RS row = center front steek sts (see page 5). Steek sts are always worked in a single color and are not included in stitch counts. Change to larger circular and join to work in the round. Pm at each side with 43 (49, 55, 61) sts for each front and 94 (106, 118, 130) sts for the back. Work around in stockinette and Pattern A until piece measures approx. 10¾ (11, 11½, 11¾) in / 27 (28, 29, 30) cm. End as shown on the chart. Work Pattern B followed by 1 rnd with Color 3, binding off 8 sts centered at each side for the armholes = 4 sts bound off on each side of each side marker = 39 (45, 51, 57) sts rem for each front and 86 (98, 110, 122) sts for the back. Set body aside while you make the sleeves.

Sleeves
With Color 1 and smaller dpn, CO 48 (48, 52, 52) sts. Divide sts onto dpn and join. Work around in k2, p2 ribbing for 1½ in / 4 cm. Change to larger dpn. Continue around in stockinette and Pattern C. See the arrow for the center of the sleeve and count back to determine where to begin the pattern for your size. Shape sleeve approx. every 2 in / 5 cm. Increase with M1: K1, M1, knit until 1 sts rem, M1, k1. Increase a total of 14 (15, 14, 15) times = 76 (78, 80, 82) sts. *At the same time,* after completing Pattern C, work Pattern A until the sleeve measures

approx. 13¾ (14¼, 14½, 15) in / 35 (36, 37, 38) cm or until 4 in / 10 cm before desired total sleeve length. End at the same pattern rnd as for the body. Work Pattern B followed by 1 rnd with Color 3, binding off 8 sts at underarm = 4 sts bound off on each side of marker = 68 (70, 72, 74) sts rem. Set sleeve aside and make the second sleeve the same way.

Raglan Shaping
Place all the pieces onto larger circular, working around with Color 3, with k2tog joining last and first sts between each piece = 4 decreases around = 296 (324, 352, 380) sts total. Pm around each of the 4 joined sts at intersections of body and sleeves—4 marked sts. Knit 2 (2, 4, 4) more rnds with Color 3. Now work 2 rnds of the rose pattern. Note that the pattern will not align at the center front or at the marked sts. Continue with the rose pattern and, *at the same time,* always knit each marked st with Color 3 while shaping raglan as follows: *knit until 2 sts before first marked st, ssk, k1 (= marked st), k2tog*. Rep from * to * at each marked st = 8 sts decreased on rnd. Rep the decrease rnd on every other rnd a total of 20 (21, 22, 23) times. After completing the rose pattern, continue with Color 3 only. *At the same time,* place the 4 steek sts + 10 (11, 12, 13) sts on each side of the steek on a holder for front neck. Work back and forth and place another 3 sts onto holder at the beginning of every row, continuing raglan shaping as est on the back and as long as possible on the front. When a total of 28 (29, 30, 31) raglan decrease rnds/rows have been worked on the back, BO rem sts.

Finishing
Gently steam press garment. Machine stitch 2 lines on each side of the center st of the front steek. Carefully cut steek open down center st.

174

Left Front Band

With Color 1 and smaller circular, pick up and knit 3 sts for every 4 rows along the left front edge. The stitch count must be a multiple of 4. Work back and forth as follows:

Row 1 (WS): K1 (edge st, (p2, k2) until 3 sts rem and end with p2, k1 (edge st).
Row 2 (RS): K1 (edge st, (k2, p2) until 3 sts rem and end with k2, k1 (edge st).
Rep these 2 rows until piece measures approx. 1½ in / 4 cm. Loosely BO in ribbing.

Right Front Band

Work as for left front band, with 6 buttonholes evenly spaced on the 4th row. The bottom buttonhole should be approx. 1¼ in / 3 cm above the cast-on row and the top one about 1¼ in / 3 cm down from neck. Place the rem buttonholes evenly spaced in between. The last 2 buttonholes will be made in the neckband.
Buttonhole: BO 2 sts and, on the following row, CO 2 sts over the gap.

Neckband

With Color 1 and smaller circular, pick up and knit 3 sts for every 4 rows along the neck and front bands = approx. 112 (116, 120, 124) sts. The stitch count must be a multiple of 4. Work back and forth as follows:

Row 1 (WS): K1 (edge st, (p2, k2) until 3 sts rem and end with p2, k1 (edge st).
Row 2 (RS): K1 (edge st, (k2, p2) until 3 sts rem and end with k2, k1 (edge st).
Rep these 2 rows until piece measures approx. 7 in / 18 cm. *At the same time,* don't forget to make the buttonholes: place the first one after ¾ in / 2 cm and the second one after 2¾ in / 7 cm = half of the collar. Make matching buttonholes at 4¼ in / 11 cm and 6¼ in / 16 cm so the buttonholes will meet when the neckband is folded in half.
Buttonholes: Place above buttonholes of front band: BO 2 sts and, on the following row, CO 2 sts over the gap.

Color 1: Black
Color 2: Green
Color 3: Dusty Green
Color 4: Natural
Color 5: Burgundy held together with Strawberry Red

Pattern C

center, top   repeat
of sleeve

Pattern B

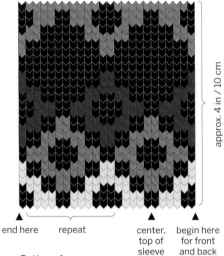

approx. 4 in / 10 cm

end here   repeat   center,   begin here
                          top of   for front
                          sleeve   and back

Pattern A

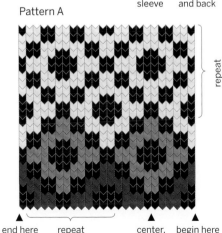

end here   repeat   center,   begin here
                          top of   for front
                          sleeve   and back

After completing band as described above, loosely BO in ribbing. Fold in half and sew down smoothly on the WS. Seam the short sides of the neckband.

Seam underarms.
Sew on buttons.
Weave in all ends neatly on WS.

Facing

If desired, you can add facings to cover the cut edges at the center front. With Color 1 and smaller circular, pick up and knit approx. 22 sts per 4 in / 10 cm on the inside of the front band. Work back and forth in stockinette for approx. ⅝ in / 1.5 cm and then BO. Turn the facing over the cut edge and sew down smoothly.

Alternatively, you can make the facing separately and sew it to the WS of the jacket over the cut edges.

Rose Pattern

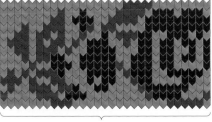

repeat

ANNA SOFÍA

A soft hat with silk ribbon ties, knitted
in alpaca-wool and silk-mohair yarns.
The motif is a women's national costume
pattern that often appears on bodices. The
hat is a modern take on the many bonnets
lavishly described by Tailor Debes in his
stories.

Sizes
One size

Materials
Yarn:
CYCA #4 (worsted, afghan, Aran)
Sandnes Garn Silk Mohair (60% kid mohair, 25% silk, 15% wool, 306 yd/280 m / 50 g)
CYCA #4 (worsted, afghan, Aran)
Sandnes Garn Alpakka Ull (65% alpaca, 35% wool, 109 yd/100 m / 50 g)

Color Suggestions:
Color 1: Silk Mohair: Ink Blue 6863 + Alpakka ull: Navy Blue 5575
Color 2: Alpakka Ull: Red 4219
Color 3: Alpakka Ull: Putty 1015

Yarn Amounts:
Sweater:
Color 1: Silk Mohair: 50 g + Alpakka ull: 50 g
Color 2: Alpakka Ull: 50 g
Color 3: Alpakka Ull: 50 g

Notions
Silk ribbon, dark blue, ⅝ in / 1.5 cm wide and approx. 31½ in / 80 cm long
Grosgrain ribbon, dark blue, 1 in / 2.5 cm wide and approx. 31½ in / 80 cm long

Needles
U.S. sizes 8 / 5 mm: short circular and U.S. size 10 / 6 mm: short circular and set of 5 dpn

Gauge
18 sts in stockinette on larger needles = 4 in / 10 cm
Adjust needle sizes to obtain correct gauge if necessary.

With Color 1 (= 1 strand of each yarn held together) and smaller circular, CO 120 sts. Work back and forth as follows:
Row 1 (WS): K1 (edge st, (p2, k2) until 3 sts rem and end with p2, k1 (edge st).
Row 2 (RS): K1 (edge st, (k2, p2) until 3 sts rem and end with k2, k1 (edge st).
Rep these 2 rows until piece measures approx. 1½ in / 4 cm. End with a WS row. Change to larger circular and begin working in stockinette and Pattern A. *At the same time*, on the 1st row, pm after and pm before the 18 outermost sts at each side, also increasing 1 st at approx. the center of the row = 121 sts. Work the next WS row.

NOTE: As you work Pattern A, decreases begin at the sides and at the markers within the piece. The chart for Pattern A does not show the decreases at the sides or at the markers. Make sure that you always have at least 2 sts in Color 1 at the beginning and end of each row and end the pattern so that it stays consistent with the stitch count inside these sts at each side. When deceasing at the markers inside the piece, it will look best if you knit with Color 1 instead of having 2 red blocks close to each other at the side.

On the next RS row, work as follows: K2tog tbl, knit until 2 sts before marker, k2tog, work to next marker, sl m and k2tog tbl. Knit until 2 sts rem on row and k2tog = 4 sts decreased across row. Work WS row in pattern. Continue working back and forth the same way, with decreases on RS rows until 89 sts rem and the last row is on the RS. Now join to work in the round. Place the last st back on the left needle and knit it + the next st together = 88 sts rem. The rnds begin here.
Continue around in Pattern A until the pattern is complete and then work with Color 1 only until there are 16 rnds total from the join for working in the rnd.

On the next rnd, begin shaping crown:
Decrease Rnd 1: (K9, k2tog) around = 8 sts decreased = 80 sts rem.
Knit 1 rnd.
Decrease Rnd 2: (K8, k2tog) around = 72 sts rem.
Knit 1 rnd.
Decrease on every other rnd as est with 1 less st between decreases until 48 sts rem.
Now decrease as est on every rnd until 16 sts rem.
(K2tog) around. Cut yarn, draw end through rem sts and tighten.
Weave in all ends neatly on WS.

Finishing
Lay the silk band over the grosgrain band, cut each to 15¾ in / 40 cm length and sew securely to the inside of each short side at the lower edge of the ribbing. Trim the bands diagonally.

Color 1: Ink Blue + Navy Blue
Color 2: Red
Color 3: Putty

Pattern A

▲ end here   repeat 13 times   begin here ▲

MARIA CHRISTINA

A long flowing women's jacket with a shawl
collar and large pockets. This pattern is
knitted with a blend of alpaca-silk and
tweed yarns, and features women's national
costume motifs on half of the body. It was
inspired by one of Tailor Debes's stories
about a banished lady-in-waiting who had
to flee to the Faroe Islands when the queen
of Denmark was imprisoned in 1772.

Sizes
S-M (L- XL)

Finished Measurements
Chest: 44 (48) in / 112 (122) cm
Length, back: 37½ (40¼) in / 95 (102) cm
Sleeve length, above fold: 21 (21¼) in / 53 (54) cm including 2¾ in / 7 cm upturned cuff or desired length
All measurements refer to the finished garment sizing and are calculated with the listed gauge.

Materials
Yarn:
CYCA #1 (fingering) Sandnes Garn Alpaca Silk (70% baby alpaca, 30% mulberry silk, 218 yd/199 m / 50 g)
CYCA #5 (bulky) Sandnes Garn Tweed (40% baby alpaca, 32% viscose, 20% nylon, 8% Merino wool, 164 yd/150 m / 50 g)

Color Suggestions:
Color 1: Alpaca Silk: Ink Blue 6063 + Tweed: Navy Blue 5585
Color 2: Alpaca Silk: Light Gray Heather 1042 + Tweed: Gray 1054

Yarn Amounts:
Color 1:
Alpaca Silk: 350 (400) g
Tweed: 500 (600) g
Color 2:
Alpaca Silk: 50 (50) g
Tweed: 100 (100) g

Needles
U.S. sizes 8 and 9 / 5 and 5.5 mm: Circulars and sets of 5 dpn

Gauge
17 sts in stockinette on larger needles = 4 in / 10 cm
Adjust needle sizes to obtain correct gauge if necessary.

184

NOTE: If you knit single color stockinette more loosely than two-color pattern knitting, use needles one U.S. or one-half metric size smaller when working in stockinette.

Front and Back
With Color 1 (= 1 strand of each yarn held together) and larger circular, CO 142 (150) sts. Pm at each side with 96 (104) sts for the back and 23 (23) sts for each front. Work back and forth in stockinette. *At the same time*, at the end of every row, CO 5,4,2,2,2,1,1,1 (6,5,3,2,2,1,1,1) sts. Next, increase 1 st at the end of every other row (3 (4) times at each side = 21 (25) sts total at each side = 44 (48) sts for each front and a total of 184 (200) sts. Continue without further increasing until the piece measures 13¾ (15¾) in / 35 (40) cm.
On the next RS row, set aside sts for pockets: Knit the first 15 (19) sts; *knit the next 29 sts with a smooth contrast-color waste yarn. Move the pocket sts back to left needle and knit with Color 1*. Knit to marker on left side and then work the next 29 sts as for * to *. Knit the last 15 (19) sts of row. Purl next row.

At this point, join to work jacket in the round. CO 4 sts at the end of the WS row just finished = center front steek sts (see page 5). Steek sts are always worked in a single color and are not included in stitch counts. Now work Pattern A around until piece measures 20½ (22½) in / 52 (57) cm.
Begin Shaping V-neck: Decrease 1 st at each side of the center front steek approx. every 1¼ (1¼-1⅜) in / 3 (3-3.5) cm a total of 13 times on each side. *At the same time*, when the piece measures 28¾ (30¾) in / 73 (78) cm, begin shaping armholes at each side: BO 4 sts on each side of each side marker = 8 sts decreased at each

side. On the next rnd, CO 4 new sts over each gap = armhole steek sts (see page 5). Steek sts are always worked in a single color and are not included in stitch counts. Continue shaping armholes at each side of the steek on every other rnd = 2,2,1,1,1,1 (2,2,1,1,1,1,1) sts. When armhole measures 8¾ (9½) in / 22 (24) cm, all the V-neck shaping should be complete and 19 (22) sts rem for each shoulder on the front. There is no binding off for back neck. BO all rem sts.

Sleeves
With Color 1 (= 1 strand of each yarn held together) and smaller dpn, CO 40 (42) sts. Divide sts onto dpn and join. Work garter st in the round: purl 1 rnd, knit 1 rnd until there are 3 ridges (5 rnds). Change to larger dpn and continue around in stockinette. Every 1½ (1¼) in / 4 (3.5) cm, increase as follows: K1, M1, knit until 1 st rem, M1, k1. Increase the same way a total of 11 (12) times = 62 (66) sts. When sleeve measures given or desired length, BO 8 sts centered at underarm.

Now work back and forth in stockinette and BO 2 sts at the beginning of every row 2 times on each side. Next, decrease 1 st at the beginning of every row until 24 (28) sts rem. BO 2 sts at the beginning of every row 2 times on each side. BO rem 16 (20) sts. Make the other sleeve the same way.

Finishing
Gently steam press the sweater. Measure and mark the depth of armhole—8¾ (9½) in / 22 (24) cm. Machine stitch armhole on each side of the center st of steek. Carefully cut open armhole down the center stitch between the machine-stitching. Reinforce and cut center front steek the same way. Seam shoulders.

Collar

The collar is worked holding 2 strands of Tweed Color 1 with 1 strand of Alpaca Silk Color 1 (= 3 strands held together). The collar is made in two pieces which will be sewn together at the back neck. With RS facing, the 3 strands of yarn, and larger circular, pick up and knit approx. 83 (89) sts. Make sure that the stitch count is a multiple of 2+1. Begin picking up at the base of the V-neck on the right front and continuing to the center of back neck. Pick up sts a bit closer together at back neck so that the collar will be full here. Work 1 row of k1, p1 ribbing on WS, from the center back neck. Turn and work knit over knit and purl over purl. When collar measures 3/8 in / 1 cm, begin shaping it at the front by working short rows: When 3 sts rem on the row down at the base of V-neck, turn and sl the 1st st. Work back in ribbing to the center of back neck. On the next row, work until 6 sts rem; turn and sl the 1st st. Continue in short rows, with 3 fewer sts on the row for each turn, until collar is approx. 9½ in / 24 cm wide at center back. Work 1 row in ribbing over all the sts and then loosely BO in ribbing on next row.

Work the other side of the collar the same way, reversing shaping to match. Begin picking up sts at the center back, with RS facing.
Neatly seam the collar pieces at center back neck.

Edging along Lower Edge of Jacket

Work a garter st edging from the base of the V-neck on the left side, along the left edge and curve, along back, along the right curve, and up to the beginning of the V-neck on the right side.

Beginning on left side, with edge to edge at the end of the V-neck, with RS facing, smaller circular, and Color 1 (1 strand of each yarn held together), pick up and knit about 17-18 sts per 4 in / 10 cm. Pick up a few extra sts along the curves so that the edge doesn't draw in but stays nice and rounded. Pick up sts until about edge-to-edge with the base of neck on right side = 1 knit row. Knit 5 rows back and forth and then BO loosely on the next RS row = 3 ridges. Sew the short ends of the base of V-neck on each side. Draw the edge a little together with the sewing thread because it is a little wider than the edge of the V-neck.

Facing inside the Jacket

With Color 1 and smaller circular, pick up and knit about 17-18 sts per 4 in / 10 cm along the inside of the right side at beginning of the cut edge. Work back and forth in stockinette for 3 rows and then BO. Work the left side the same way. Turn the facings over the cut edges and sew down so the right side of facings faces out.

Pockets

Insert a larger dpn into the sts below the waste yarn and another dpn into the sts above the waste yarn. Carefully remove waste yarn. Divide the sts onto 4 dpn and, with Color 1, work around in stockinette for 7 in / 18 cm. BO. Sew the lower edges of pockets down on WS of body.

Attach Sleeves

Pin each sleeve around armhole, centered at the shoulder seam and at underarm. Beginning at shoulder seam, sew down each side separately.

Facing around Sleeve Top

For a finished look on the WS, you can knit a facing around the sleeve top to cover the cut edges around armhole. With smaller circular and 1 strand of Tweed Color 1, pick up and knit approx. 7 sts per 2 in / 5 cm, from the center of underarm and all around the armhole. Work so that RS of facing will show on the outside when turned to cover the cut edges. Working back and forth, work 3 rows in stockinette and then BO loosely. Sew down facing on WS.

Weave in all ends neatly on WS.

185

Color 1: Ink Blue + Navy Blue
Color 2: Light Gray Heather + Gray

Pattern A

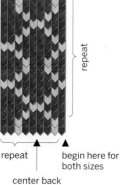

repeat

repeat

begin here for both sizes

center back

TOVA PONCHO

A large, roomy poncho, knitted in alpaca and silk-mohair yarns. In the front, there's an opening for a child in a baby carrier. This pattern combines the motifs *krúnan* ("crown"), *gásareygað* ("goose eye"), and *puntarnir* ("squares"). The baby hat uses the same yarn and pattern.

"One popular pattern was *krúnan*, *gásareygað*, and *puntarnir*. This pattern was all the rage when I was young. Many would knit for themselves, always cardigans. That pattern was frequently used, in natural hues."

Tova, age 87

Sizes
Poncho: One size
Baby Hat: 3 (6-9, 12) months

Finished Measurements
Poncho:
Circumference around shoulders: approx. 47¼ in / 120 cm
Circumference around lower edge: approx. 87 in / 222 cm
Length: approx. 32¼ in / 82 cm or desired length
All measurements refer to the finished garment sizing and are calculated with the listed gauge.

MATERIALS
Yarn:
CYCA #3 (DK, light worsted) Sandnes Garn Alpaca (100% alpaca, 120 yd/110 m / 50 g)
CYCA #4 (worsted, afghan, Aran) Sandnes Garn Silk Mohair (60% kid mohair, 25% silk, 15% wool, 306 yd/280 m / 50 g)

Color Suggestions:
Color 1: Alpaca: Dark Gray Heather 1053 + Silk Mohair: Black 1099
Color 2: Alpaca: Gray Heather 1042 + Silk Mohair: Natural 1012
Color 3: Alpaca: Corn Yellow 2015 + Silk Mohair: Natural 1012
Color 4: Alpaca: Natural 1012 + Silk Mohair: Natural 1012

Yarn Amounts:
Poncho:
Color 1: Alpaca: 600 g + Silk Mohair: 200 g
Color 2: Alpaca: 50 g + Silk Mohair: 100 g (also used with colors 3 and 4 in Alpaca)
Color 3: Alpaca: 50 g + Silk Mohair: -
Color 4: Alpaca: 150 g + Silk Mohair: -

Baby Hat:
Color 1: Alpaca: 50 g
All other colors: 50 g of each color or leftovers from poncho

Needles
U.S. sizes 8 and 9 / 5 and 5.5 mm: Circulars

Notions
8 small press buttons for the opening at center front

Gauge
18 sts in stockinette on larger needles = 4 in / 10 cm
Adjust needle sizes to obtain correct gauge if necessary.

NOTE: If you knit single color stockinette more loosely than two-color pattern knitting, use needles one U.S. or one-half metric size smaller when working in stockinette.

TIPS FOR INCREASES
In this pattern, increases are made with a yarnover between two sts. On the next rnd, work the yarnover as k1tbl (work into back rather than front of st), to avoid holes.

PONCHO

The poncho is worked in the round, from the top down. With Color 4 (= 1 strand of each yarn held together) and larger circular, CO 100 sts. Join, being careful not to twist cast-on row. Pm for beginning of rnd. Work around in k2, p2 ribbing until piece measures approx. 8 in / 20 cm. Change to smaller circular and decrease 20 sts evenly spaced around = 80 sts rem. Now work around in k1, p1 ribbing until neck measures approx. 10¼ in / 26 cm. From this rnd on, work around in stockinette; all subsequent measurements are taken from this point. Change to larger circular. Knit 1 rnd, increasing 34 sts evenly spaced around (see Tips for Increases above) = 114 sts. Knit 1 rnd without increasing. Next, increase 34 sts evenly spaced around = 148 sts. Pm at beginning of rnd = right shoulder/side of poncho.

Work *k10, p1, k2, p1, k45, p1, k2, p1, k11*. Rep from * to * once more. Pm around the groups of 4 sts worked as p1, k2, p1 = 4 marked sts for increases. On the next rnd, begin the increases. Increase (as described above) on each side of the sets of 4 marked sts = 8 sts increased per round. Knit the increased sts. There will be 2 more sts between each marker for each increase rnd. Repeat the increases every 4th rnd. Work until piece measures 2¾ in / 7 cm (from rnd beginning stockinette section). Work Pattern A in the round. Note the arrows for the center front, center back, and center of shoulders and count out to the side to determine where to begin the pattern. Continue increasing as est, but work p1, k2, p1 with MC of pattern (first with Color 2 and then with Color 1). Work the new sts into pattern as well as possible. After completing Pattern A, work the rest of the poncho with Color 1. On the 2nd rnd with Color 1, use a smooth contrast-color waste yarn to set off the opening at center front (if you don't want an opening at center front, skip the waste yarn instructions that follow). With the waste yarn, knit the center 45 sts of front. Slip the sts back to left needle and work the sts with Color 1. Continue around as est. Increase a total of 11 times= 236 sts. Now increase on every 4th rnd, in towards the front, 28 times (= 56 sts increased). *At the same time*, along the shoulders and on the back, increase on every 6th rnd 18 times = 108 sts increased = 400 sts total. Now work around without increasing until poncho is approx. 32¼ in / 82 cm or desired length. If you want to finish before the given length, you can begin the ribbing at the lower edge even if you haven't worked as many increases as specified. Change to smaller circular. Work 3 rnds of k1, p1 ribbing. Loosely BO in ribbing. Gently steam press poncho.

Front Opening
Insert the smaller circular into the sts below the waste yarn and then move needle to insert into the sts above waste yarn (or use two circulars). Carefully remove waste yarn. With Color 1 (1 strand of each yarn held together), BO the sts on top of the opening. With Color 1, work in k1, p1 ribbing back and forth over the sts below opening for about 2 in / 5 cm and then BO in ribbing.

Sew some press buttons on the inside of the opening for closure.

"Sleeves"
Lay the poncho flat and pm at the outermost st on the lower edge of

the ribbing at each side (= centered between the raglan increases at the sides). With Color 1 (= 1 strand of each yarn held together) and smaller circular, pick up and knit 15 sts on each side of the marked sts = 31 sts total. Work back and forth in k1, p1 ribbing until the "sleeve" measures approx. 8¾ in / 22 cm. BO in ribbing. Sew the sleeve together along the sides and fold double. Make a "sleeve" the same way on the opposite side.

Weave in all ends neatly on WS.

BABY HAT
With Color 1 (1 strand of each yarn held together), and smaller circular, CO 51 (55, 59) sts. Purl 1 row on WS and, *at the same time*, pm after 19 (20, 21) sts and after 32 (35, 38) sts. There should be 13 (15, 17) sts between the markers. Begin Pattern B with the first row on the RS. Work back and forth in stockinette and pattern. *At the same time*, increase 1 st after the first and before the last marker on each RS row about every 1¼ (1, ¾) in / 3 (2.5, 2) cm, 2 (3, 4) times at each marker = 4 (6, 8) sts increased for a total of 55 (61, 67) sts. Work until piece measures approx. 3¼ (3½, 4) in / 8 (9, 10) cm. All subsequent measurements are taken from this point. BO the first and last 19 (20, 21) sts on the next RS row. Continue in pattern, working back and forth over the center 17 (21, 25) sts, until the piece (= the middle section) is as long as the bound-off sides. BO rem sts.

Finishing
Sew the side sections to the center part.

Edging along Lower Edge of Hat
Begin with the RS on the left side and, with Color 1 (1 strand of each yarn held together) and smaller circular, pick up and knit sts along the lower edge—about 1 st in each st. Work back and forth in stockinette. *At the same time*, decrease approx. 10 (12, 14) sts

evenly spaced across the first row. Work as est until the edging measures approx. ¾ in / 2 cm and then BO. The edging should roll up with the garter ridges upwards. Sew a few small stitches to tack the top of the rolled edge where stitches were picked up = casing for the cord.

Edging along Face Opening
Pick up and knit about 1 st in every row/st around the face as for the lower edge. Work back and forth in stockinette. *At the same time*, decrease approx. 6 (8, 10) sts evenly spaced across the first row. Work as est until the edging measures approx. ¾ in / 2 cm and then BO. The edging should roll up with the garter ridges upwards. Do not tack the edging.

With Color 1 doubled, twist a cord about 23¾ in / 60 cm long when fully twisted. Thread the cord through the casing at lower edge. Make two tassels and attach securely to the ends of the cord.

Weave in all ends neatly on WS.

193

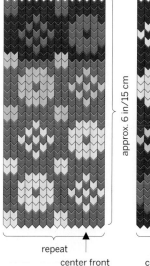

- Color 1: Dark Gray Heather + Black
- Color 2: Gray Heather + Natural
- Color 3: Corn Yellow + Natural
- Color 4: Natural + Natural

Pattern A   Pattern B

repeat

approx. 6 in/15 cm

repeat   repeat

center front
center back
center of each shoulder

center
back of
hat

SKÓLEISTAR—
KNITTED HOUSE SLIPPERS

Skóleistar are soft shoe liners that double as slippers, knitted here in a blend of wool and silk-mohair. The four pattern variations are composed of different motifs from Tailor Debes's book. There is a long-standing tradition of knitted *skóleistar* in the Faroes, made from Faroese wool and worn inside wooden clogs or rubber shoes. Nowadays they're used as house slippers. When you're visiting older Faroese people, you'll often be asked if you'd like to borrow a pair of *skóleistar* to keep your feet warm—a lovely display of hospitality that has survived into this millenium.

"People also wear knitted wool shoes, which are not stitched through, inside ordinary shoes, and they are called *skóleistar*."

Svabo 1782

Sizes

One size (fits shoe sizes approx. U.S. 7-9 / Euro 37-39)

Finished Measurements

Length of sole: approx. 9 in / 23 cm when lightly stretched
All measurements refer to the finished garment sizing and are calculated with the listed gauge.

Materials
Yarn:

CYCA #1 (fingering) Sandnes Garn Sisu (80% wool, 20% nylon, 191 yd/175 m / 50 g)
CYCA #4 (worsted, afghan, Aran) Sandnes Garn Silk Mohair (60% kid mohair, 25% silk, 15% wool, 306 yd/280 m / 50 g)
OR
CYCA #2 (sport, baby) Sandnes Garn Tresko (80% wool, 20% nylon, 115 yd/105 m / 50 g)

Color Suggestions:
Version 1:
Color 1: Sisu: Powder Pink 3511 + Silk Mohair: Powder Pink 3511
Color 2: Sisu: Light Beige Heather 3021 + Silk Mohair: Sand 2521

Version 2:
Color 1: Sisu: Black 1099 + Silk Mohair: Black 1099
Color 2: Sisu: Natural 1012 + Silk Mohair: Natural 1012

Version 3:
Color 1: Sisu: Navy Blue 5575 + Silk Mohair: Ink Blue 6863

Color 2: Sisu: Red 4228 + Silk Mohair: Strawberry Red 4065

Version 4:
Color 1: Sisu: Corn Yellow 2015 + Silk Mohair: Acid Yellow 2005
Color 2: Sisu: Light Gray Heather 1032 + Silk Mohair: Light Gray 1032

Yarn Amounts:
Color 1: 50 g of each color
Color 2: 50 g of each color

The slippers can also be knitted with Tresko yarn. See the photo of the red and black slippers on the previous page. 1 strand of Tresko = the same weight as 1 strand Sisu + 1 strand Silk Mohair held together

Needles

U.S. size 4 / 3.5 mm: set of 5 dpn

Crochet Hook

U.S. size D-3 / 3 mm, if you want to crochet around the top edges

Gauge

22 sts in stockinette = 4 in / 10 cm
Adjust needle size to obtain correct gauge if necessary.

With Color 1 (= 1 strand of each yarn held together) and dpn, CO 7 sts. Working back and forth, work 19 rows in stockinette, following the chart of the pattern you've selected.
NOTE: The first and last rows of the heel are on the WS.
Cut yarn.

Now pick up and knit sts along each side of the heel. The 9 heel sts are at the center back but the chart is drawn so it clearly shows how the slippers will look on the top and bottom sides. Note the arrow on the chart which indicates where the row begins and ends on the RS. Beginning at the top of the right side, with RS facing, pick up and knit 16 sts in pattern along the heel, work the 9 heel sts in pattern, pick up and knit 16 sts in pattern along the left side = 41 sts total.

For Patterns B and D: The first 2 and last 2 sts are always knit on all rows = edge sts. Continue working back and forth as shown on the charts until you've increased 2 times at each side at top center of the foot = 45 sts. Note the arrow at the side of the chart which indicates where you will begin working in the round.

Cut yarn. The rnds begin as indicated by the arrow at the side of the chart. Don't forget to cast on the last new st at the top center of the foot on this rnd = 46 sts. Work the rest of the slipper in the round and BO for the toe as shown on the chart = 10 sts rem. Cut yarn, draw end through rem sts and tighten.

Make a second slipper the same way.

Weave in all ends neatly on WS.

200

Edging Alternatives for the Top of the Slippers

Garter Stitch Edging
With Color 1 and dpn, pick up and knit about 22 sts per 4 in / 10 cm around the top opening of the slipper. Purl 1 rnd, knit 1 rnd, purl 1 rnd. BO the next rnd knitwise.

Rolled Edging
With Color 1 and dpn, pick up and knit about 22 sts per 4 in / 10 cm around the top opening of the slipper. Knit around in stockinette for 1¼-1½ in / 3-4 cm. BO knitwise.

Crocheted Edging
With Color 1 and crochet hook, make 2 rnds of single crochet (= British double crochet) around top of slipper. Fasten off.

You can make larger slippers by making extra stripes at the sides and adding more length as needed before shaping the toe.

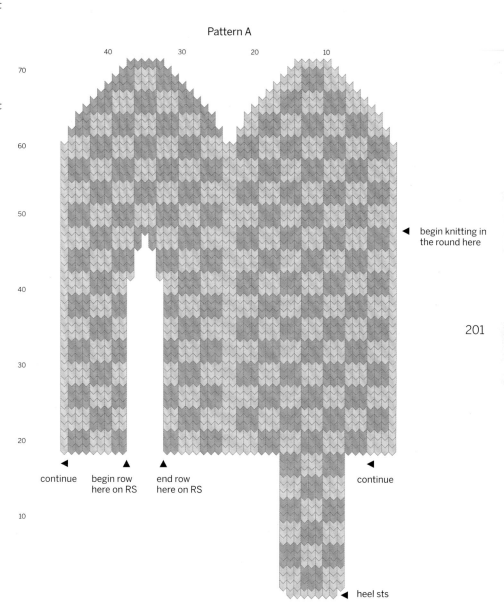

Pattern A

begin knitting in the round here

continue   begin row here on RS   end row here on RS   continue

heel sts

201

Version 1
Color 1: Powder Pink + Powder Pink
Color 2: Light Beige Heather + Sand

Pattern B

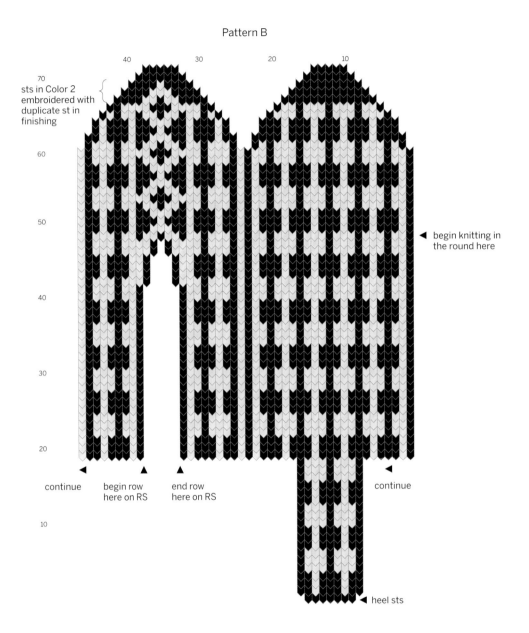

70

sts in Color 2
embroidered with
duplicate st in
finishing

◀ begin knitting in
the round here

202

continue   begin row   end row   continue
                here on RS   here on RS

◀ heel sts

Version 2
 Color 1: Black + Black
 Color 2: Natural + Natural

Pattern C

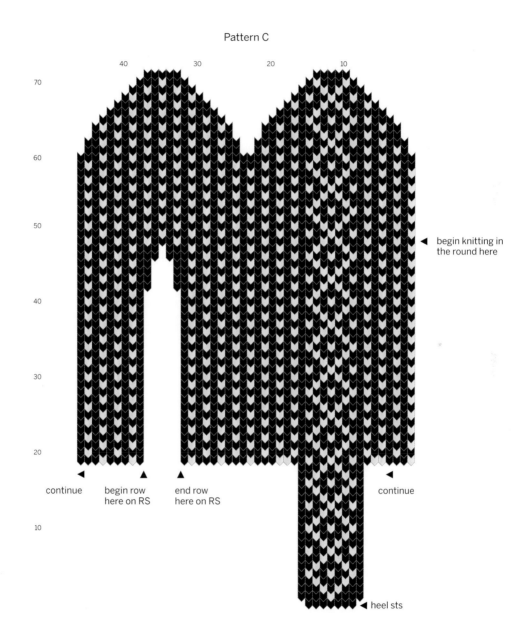

begin knitting in
the round here

203

continue   begin row   end row   continue
            here on RS   here on RS

heel sts

Version 2
Color 1: Black + Black
Color 2: Natural + Natural

Pattern D

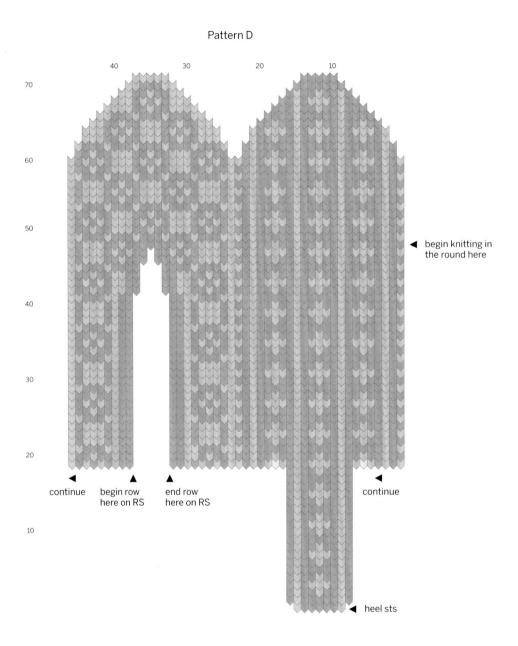

begin knitting in
the round here

continue | begin row here on RS | end row here on RS | continue

heel sts

Version 3
 Color 1: Navy + Ink Blue
Color 2: Red + Strawberry Red

Version 4
Color 1: Corn Yellow + Acid Yellow
Color 2: Light Gray Heather + Light Gray

ACKNOWLEDGMENTS

Thank you to all our knitters. Thank you for the days and evenings spent crafting this book, stitch by stitch, with your caring hands.

Alma Elmelund Andreassen
Andrea á Rípuni
Anna Havmand
Anna Petersen
Anne Marie Lid
Elinborg á Lofti
Fridrikka Joensen
Gudny Vang
Henrikka Øregaard
Herborg Haraldsen
Herdis Jacobsen
Ingebjørg Sivertsen
Janett Vatle Berntzen
Jóna Maria Poulsen
Jórun Simonsen
Karin S. Hansen
Katrin Hansen
Lone B. Eriksdóttir
Rakul Biskopstø
Randi Jacobsen
Siv Dyvik
Siv Hesjedal
Vibeke Gerlach Ingvarsson
Åse Hauge
Åshild Bakke

With thanks to

Sandnes Garn
Gry Geelmuyden
Siv Dyvik
Anette Evensen

Fridrikka Joensen
Tova Jacobsen
Maria Klein

Heðin Klein
Theodor Hansen
Annfinnur Zachariassen
Elbjørn Joensen

Lise Finne
Bjørg Sandvik
Anna Havmand
Elinborg á Lofti
Marita Guttesen

Óli Jacobsen
Viggo Christiansen

Áki Davidsen
Eyðun Jørgensen
Barbara Chaparro

Models

Annika Steintórsdóttir
Biskopstø
Armgarð Mortensen
Aura Elisabet Thomsen
Bjørt Hoydal Joensen
Ingibjørg Mortensen
Jónrid Biskopstø Sivertsen
Levi Joensen
Mari Hamrá
Maria Friis
Pætur Zachariasson
Tord Strøm Rødland
Yngvi

Place Names

The photos in this book were
taken in these places in the
Faroe Islands.

Í Norðradali
Í Gerðum
Kvívík
Fossá
Eiðisskarði
Fitjum
Úti á Reyni
Tinganesi
Kýrbergi
Vágsbotni
Í Gongini
Leynum
Tjørnuvík
Hálsinum
Norðradalsskarði
Við Toftavatn
Við Gjógv
Við Bryggjubakka
Undir Svartafossi

YARN INFORMATION

LoveKnitting.com
www.loveknitting.com/us

If you are unable to obtain any of the yarn used in this book, it can be replaced with a yarn of a similar weight and composition. Please note, however, the finished projects may vary slightly from those shown, depending on the yarn used. Try www.yarnsub.com for suggestions.

For more information on selecting or substituting yarn, contact your local yarn shop or an online store; they are familiar with all types of yarns and would be happy to help you. Additionally, the online knitting community at Ravelry.com has forums where you can post questions about specific yarns. Yarns come and go so quickly these days and there are so many beautiful yarns available.